PIRATE TRIALS:

Hung By the Neck until Dead

KEN ROSSIGNOL

KEN ROSSIGNOL

Introduction

"We showed no mercy,
None should be shown for us"

Those who committed shocking murders and plundered merchant ships on the high seas have been glamourized in movies, television and books for hundreds of years. This book will not feed into that fantasy but instead brings forth facts.

PIRATE TRIALS: Hung by the neck until dead, brings to life the harsh reality of the crimes and the times when piracy was rampant. These selected stories are told through actual news reports and the detailed records and reports of the indictments and trials of some of the most bloodthirsty criminals ever to sail the seven seas.

In some cases, the last words, dying declarations and repentant remarks as uttered by those facing the gallows are included. Descriptions of how the executions took place may be graphic and shocking to some readers but they are no more shocking that what form of torture and violent death were administered to their victims.

The first such 'Dying Declarations of Nicholas Fernandez' gives a first person account of his own participation into countless acts of horror, the likes of which are never portrayed in the flicks put out by Hollywood. The personification of evil as accounted for by this man on his way to the gallows is as spellbinding today as to those who heard his words as he awaited his fate of being hung, dragged, drawn and quartered. Even the fires of Hell will never repay him and his shipmates for their crimes that he so adequately describes and lays the cause of it all on his succumbing to the Demon Rum.

Various acts of war in another case were decried by one side as piracy while treaties between England and the United States called for recognition of acts of war and international law cited the long history of Privateers in seizing ships and men. Other treaties called for extradition of criminals between England and the United States.

The legal documents and transcripts of trials in England, Canada (British North American Colonies) and the United States bring to life the actual arguments made during these various incidents of bloodshed and violence on the high seas. In addition, in some cases, actual news reports of the time were the first reporting of these acts and as available, are presented here for the modern reader.

Every effort has been made to keep language translations to a minimum in order to preserve the authenticity of the **Pirate Trials** yet explain Old English words and terms to the Twenty-First Century reader.

Many acts of piracy over the centuries involved bands of ruthless and cut-throat killers preying on merchant vessels in the Caribbean. Other pirates operated with the official blessing of the warlords and Deys of the Barbary Coast of Africa.

In the 21st century, acts of piracy occur with great frequency off the coast of Somalia. Great ships are taken prisoner and held for ransom with hostages held at gunpoint. One incident, in April of 2009, pirates off of the coast of Somalia attacked the Italian cruise liner *MSC Melody*. A privately contracted Israeli security crew returned fire after the pirates fired weapons at the bridge of the ship from a speedboat which came alongside the vessel. Passengers on the ship threw deck chairs and other items down on the pirate boat. The *Melody* attack took place about 200 miles north of the Seychelles and 500 miles east of Somalia.

Efforts to fight piracy by seafaring nations have had various degrees of success, both centuries ago as well as today. When United States President Thomas Jefferson decided to stop paying ransoms or "tributes" to the Barbary Pirates and instead send warships, soon the piracy of U. S. vessels were halted. But tributes from European powers continued into the 1830's.

Today, millions of dollars are paid on a regular basis to Somali pirates. Several of those pirates were recently convicted in United States Federal Courts on piracy charges. Others have been dispatched to the deep when armed pirates have been engaged by naval forces.

Acknowledgements

The Illustrated News of London,
The New York Times,
The British Colonist
Harper's Weekly
The Guardian
Cruise Critic
...and United States Naval Historical Center are among the sources relied upon for news of actual piratical acts involved in the stories related in this book. The Library of Congress, the British Library and the Library of Virginia are also acknowledged as sources of information for this effort.

These drawings depicted the steamer Chesapeake, top, as passengers and crew were offloaded in Nova Scotia, and bottom, underway.   Harper's Weekly.

Part One

Dying Declarations of

NICHOLAS FERNANDEZ,
Who with Nine Others were executed in front of Cadiz Harbour, December 29th, 1829

FOR

PIRACY AND MURDER

On The High Seas

With a Solemn Warning to Youth (and others) to beware of the baneful habit of INTEMPERANCE

Southern District of New York.

BE IT REMEMBERED, That on the 10th day of May A.D. Eighteen Hundred and Thirty in the 54th year of American Independence of the United States of America, George Lambert, of the said District, hath deposited in this office, the title of a Book the right where of he claims as Proprietor, in the words following, to wit—*Dying Declaration of Nicholas Fernandez,* who with nine others were Executed in front of Cadiz Harbour, Dec. 29, 1829. for piracy and murder on the high seas—translated from a Spanish copy by Ferdinand Bayer—annexed is a *Solemn Warning to Youth*, and others, to beware of the baneful habit of Intemperance.

In conformity to the Act of Congress of the United States, entitled "an Act for the encouragement of Learning, by securing the copies of Maps, Charts, and Books, the authors and proprietors of such copies, during the time therein mentioned." And also to an Act, entitled "An Act, supplementary to an Act entitled an Act for the encouragement of Learning, by securing the copies of Maps, Charts, and Books, to the authors and proprietors of such copies, daring the times therein mentioned, and extending the benefits thereof to the arts of designing, engraving, and etching historical and other prints."

FRED: J. BETTS.
Clerk of the Southern District of New York

DYING DECLARATION OF NICHOLAS FERNANDEZ, THE PIRATE.

THE mind of sensibility must feel for the situation of the relatives of the meanest malefactor but when, as in the present case, an innocent and respectable family is involved in disgrace from the vices of one, whose education ought to have ranked him as a respectable and distinguished member, we are shocked at such degeneracy.

The poignant affliction, which the infamous crimes of children bring upon their parents, ought to be one of the most effective persuasions to refrain from vice.

How dreadful must be the reflection of the condemned wretch, in the hour of an ignominious and violent death that his evil conduct will in all probability bring down the grey hairs of venerable parents with sorrow to the grave!

That such may have been the reflection of the misguided and wretched Fernandez, in his last moments, the reader will not doubt on perusing his dying declaration, which was penned during his, confinement, and by him presented to an acquaintance on the morning of his execution for publication:

"I am by birth a Spaniard, and of respectable and pious parents, who, in my early youth emigrated from old Spain to the island of Cuba, where they may be still living. I was the youngest of three sons, and although no expense or pains were spared in my education, and from a too indulgent father received encouragement that at the age of twenty-one, I should receive a patrimonial portion, sufficient to establish me in any respectable business, that I should prefer.

Setting Out to Sail the World

Yet, when but nineteen years of age, the strong inclination which I felt to travel abroad, and to see the world, outweighed every other consideration, and a opposition to the wise council and good advice of parents and friends, I privately left them, and took passage for New-Orleans.

The funds with which I had taken care in a clandestine manner to provide myself, not only there procured me respectable lodgings, but (until they became exhausted by extreme imprudence and folly) enabled me to associate with those whom I at first supposed honest and respectable—but, alas, in this I in a very few days, by sad experience, found that I had been very much deceived.

Learning the Games of Chance

No pains were spared by the designing and crafty, in whom I had placed implicit confidence, to allure me from the paths of virtue and rectitude by prevailing on me to accompany them to those haunts of vice and infantry, which in all populous cities more or less abound, and where they could the better effect their object; which was nothing less, than by fair means or foul to divest me of the little property that I then possessed, and which they succeeded in doing in a very few months, to the last fraction—.the means used was to prevail on me, young and inexperienced as I was, to drink to that excess as to produce brutal intoxication, and thereby render me incapable of taking care of myself; and then, by introducing a sham game at cards or billiards, rob me of

11

KEN ROSSIGNOL

all the cash that I might happen on such occasions to
have about me; nor was it infrequent, when being
aroused from a state of inebriation, to find myself
deserted by my artful companions, and without anything
left safe some article of clothing with which to satisfy the
demands of the not less artful master or mistress of the
house.

These vile practices, as may be supposed, soon
reduced me to a state of poverty and wretchedness, and
in a land where I had not a friend to whom I could apply
for relief, with any probability of success—and what
added to my miseries, the baneful habit of
intemperance, to which I bad become addicted by a too
frequent indulgence while in bad company, had now
become so ungovernable, that had *a* friend been found
willing to impart something to my relief, I think it very
probable that it would have been applied to the
purchase of ardent spirits, rather than bread, or any
necessary article of clothing of which I was then almost
destitute —it was to this, one of the greatest evils that
could ever befall man, that I think I may justly impute my
present woeful situation!—for at that period of distress,
Iam confident that with all my other faults, ragged and
penniless, I should have repented of my folly, and
willingly returned (like another prodigal son) to the arms
of my afflicted parents, and to that peaceful home where
I had ever been a stranger to want. O my dear youth,
attend to that admonition of a wretched, dying roan—
beware of Intemperance!
Joining a Wicked Ship of Killers
Being thus far from home, destitute of friends, and
unhappily deprived of all means of subsistence, it is not
very surprising that I should, thus situated, be found
willing to unite in any project however desperate or
wicked; or assent to any proposal made me, that could

12

promise a change of condition—I was indeed then just what the gang of desperadoes (with whom I was prevailed upon next to associate myself) wished to find me-not unwilling to engage in any enterprise, lawful or unlawful, just or otherwise, nay, to imbrue my hands in innocent blood, if property could thereby be obtained.

With this determination, I with four others, as resolute as myself (two of whom had been once under sentence of death, for piracy and pardoned) left in as private manner as possible, in November 1824, the port of New-Orleans, and the succeeding day were put on board a small but very swift sailing schooner, which lay at anchor in the Mississippi, many miles below the city, awaiting and in expectation of our arrival.

On board I was introduced to a crew composed of thirty-seven fellow adventurers, whose countenances seemed expressive of a determination in the unlawful enterprise in which they were about to engage, neither to take or give quarter, as circumstances might require.

Having now received her complement of men, the Schooner (which mounted eight guns, and contained small arms in abundance) was put with all possible dispatch in readiness for offensive operations—the cannon and small arms were well charged with grape and other shot, and the cutlasses arid knives ground to an edge

Ships with Sparse Cargo Were Unmolested

Thus prepared, we were very soon on cruising ground on the north side of Cuba, where we continued to cruise with but little success for about two weeks in which time we boarded but three vessels, one in ballast, and the other two with but indifferent cargoes, bound to

13

the United States, to which they were permitted to proceed, without any other molestation than the loss of their cabin furniture and small stores.

In the course of the fortnight we two or three times took a peep into the harbor of Havana, which I must confess, for the moment, produced in my mind serious and sorrowful reflections; as it could not fail to remind me of my peaceful home, wherein innocence I had with my friends enjoyed so many happy hours- nor could I but feel that I had much reason to reproach myself for the anxiety which my absence must naturally have caused my parents.

As these were feelings that did not well accord with the new character which I had assumed, I was enabled soon effectually to drown them with an extra glass of strong drink, of which we had plenty on board, and to which all were permitted to have free access.

Here I ought not omit mentioning, that as many have expressed their surprise that there could be found any (even among that class denominated Pirates) who, so destitute of every humane feeling, could deliberately deprive an innocent and unoffending fellow creature of life, and, as in some instances, while on their knees entreating for mercy!

No Quarter Was to Be Given

I would remark, that from what I do know by experience, but few there are that could do it, if not at a moment when in an intoxicated state; and spirituous liquors were invariably resorted to and drank plentifully of by all on board whenever a capture was made, and as soon as understood from our officers that no quarter was to be given.

In the months of December and January following, we were more fortunate in making prizes; eleven or twelve vessels (mostly American) were captured by us, bound to and from different parts of Europe and the West Indies, and some with valuable cargoes---our place of rendezvous and deposit of goods at that time, was a small island or key in the neighborhood of Cuba: our prizes were generally conveyed there, and after being disburthened of the most valuable part of (heir cargoes, were sometimes burnt and at other times scuttled, and the crews, it was thought not necessary other ways to dispose of them were sent adrift in their boats, and frequently without anything on-which they could subsist a single day—nor were all so fortunate as to escape with their lives—"dead men can tell no tales," was a common saying among us.

Slaughter by Majority Vote

As soon as we got a ship's crew in our power, a short consultation was held, and if it was the opinion of a majority that it would be better to take life than to spare it a single nod or wink from our captain was sufficient — regardless of age or sex.

All entreaties for mercy were then made in vain— we possessed not the tender feelings to be operated upon by the shrieks and expiring groans of the devoted victims!

There was rather a competition among us, who, with his own bands, should dispatch the greatest number, and in the shortest period of time.

Without any other motives than to gratify a such like hellish propensity (in our intoxicated moments) blood was not infrequently and unnecessarily shed, and many widows-and orphans probably made, when the lives of the unfortunate victims might have been spared, and without the most distant prospect of any evil

15

consequences (as regarded ourselves) resulting therefrom.

Throats of Entire Crew Slit In Twenty Minutes

Such indeed was the case of the crew of an American brig, which was unfortunately cast on sunken rocks, in the neighborhood of the place of our rendezvous, and where we had at that time goods and specie to a very considerable amount secreted.

As soon as we saw their predicament, we manned our boats and proceeded for the wreck, and as soon as we had got the terrified crew on board, and pinioned, we began to torture and torment them, in every way that our inventive faculties could suggest— sometimes drawing our knives across their throats, and then applying the point to their breasts, until we got them within a few rods of the shore, when the signal was given by our chief, for a general and instantaneous destruction of life.

In less than twenty minutes the bloody work was accomplished, with the exception of one, who after receiving a blow, broke in two the cord with which he was bound, jumped out of the boat into the water, and although closely pursued, succeeded in reaching the shore and making his escape.

We confined ourselves most of the time to our old cruising ground, to intercept vessels bound to and from Cuba, and with considerable success until the summer of 1825; when such was the increase of American cruisers thereabouts, fitted out as we were informed expressly for the purpose of ferreting out and capturing uncommissioned vessels of our character, and to afford protection to her commerce.

We thought it most prudent to seek new quarters and to try our fortune in a more southern latitude, where we made several valuable captures, and in doing which, we were obliged or pleased to shed some innocent blood.

Women and Children Were Murdered Without Care or Hesitation

In one instance there was such an inhuman and wanton destruction of life that the bare recollection of it at the moment I am writing, fills my mind with that degree of horror, as almost to chill the blood.

It was early in the morning of the 1st of February, 1826, that we fell in with a Portuguese ship, bound from Lisbon to St. Salvador, on board of which were near forty souls, including several women and children—suspecting our character, and if overpowered by us, expecting no mercy, they bravely defended themselves.

 Twice with no other weapons than their knives, they drove us from their decks, nor were they finally overpowered until they had killed three of our men, and severely wounded six more.

Revenge Vowed as Our Fellow Pirates Were Slain as Our Prey Fought Back

Our chief, as well as most on board, exasperated at the loss of their companions, breathed nothing but revenge.

We would not by way of retaliation be satisfied with anything short of the total destruction of the lives of all on board, without respect to *sex* or age!

A few light and most valuable articles found on board were thrown into our boats, and the ship then set on fire in three or four different places in her hold and cabin.; and not until the flames had so increased, that it was judged impossible for the wretched victims left on board to extinguish it, had we permission to quit the ship.

The fire in columns bursting from every port, and communicating to the sails and rigging, soon drove the poor sufferers forward, even to the extreme end of the ship's bowsprit—where, with up-lifted hands they most earnestly entreated us to spare their lives! as we had destroyed the ship's boats, all retreat was cut off, except to plunge themselves into the sea, which many did, but with no other effect than to prolong their misery for a few moments, for death was the portion of all who approached the schooner—some were shot in the water and others killed with hatchets while attempting to gain our decks!

The Shrieks & Dying Groans
of the Unhappy Victims

The shrieks and dying groans of the unhappy victims on board the burning ship, as the devouring flames approached them, were calculated to pierce the hearts of any but barbarians like ourselves, destitute of every humane feeling—in less than one hour the shrieks of the dying had ceased!—the work of death and destruction was completed, and little life was visible of the late noble ship but her bottom, burnt to the water's edge!

The melancholy scene of destruction was viewed with much apparent satisfaction by bur chief, and most of my companions—but not so by me!

It was a scene of death to which I had been unaccustomed—I could not for many days drive from my view the poor half consumed victims, male and female, wreathing and expiring in agony, and until deprived by the flames of the power of speech, begging for mercy!

Liquor aided in blocking memories of murder

I could not but view myself as one who merited death by an equal degree of torture—one, who had participated in an act of wickedness, that could not be surpassed! It was then that I from my very heart, cursed the unfortunate moment that united myself with a band of cruel and unrelenting murderers!

I blush to say, that however much I had been effected by a scene so shocking to humanity, yet it was but momentary, for by the aid of liquor was soon enabled to drive all such harrowing reflections from my mind, and to unite with my companions in wickedly mimicking the agonizing distortions of the unfortunate Portuguese, in their last expiring moments!

Satan Now In Control

Satan indeed had now the full control of me, and as one on whom the sentence of death has been passed, I am not now unwilling to say that I believe myself as unworthy to live as any one of my condemned companions.

From this until November 1827, we continued to cruise, and when opportunity presented we failed not to depredate upon the defenseless commerce of all nations, in the course of which we were several times chased by vessels of superior force, but were always so fortunate as to escape.

Naval Convoys Deprived Us of Prey

Not meeting with the good success that we formerly had, as the Indiamen and other vessels of valuable cargoes (alarmed at the increasing instances of piracy) were seldom now to be met with unless convoyed by some national ship of war, several of us on board concluded to adopt a somewhat different plan, which we believed would not only produce a very handsome addition to our general stock, but an

19

acquisition of hands, and place in our possession a larger vessel, and better calculated for our business.

Having by mutual agreement disposed of our own vessel and divided stock, I entered with eleven of Bay most resolute companions on board the Brazilian brig *Defensor de Pedra*, bound from Rio de Janeiro for the coast of Mina where we safely arrived.

On the passage, myself and companions had not been idle in preparing a plan to obtain possession of the brig.

With the assistance of some few others who had engaged to act in concert with us—on the 26th January, 1828, the captain and others of the brig's officers and hands, by whom we expected to be opposed, being on shore, we thought it the most favorable opportunity to carry our plan into effect.

Our plot in which we succeeded to our mind with no other trouble than that of sending unceremoniously to their long home or effectually disabling the few on board who attempted to question rights and exhibit symptoms of resistance.

Having now obtained complete possession of the brig, and having yet some suspicious characters left on board we gave them a boat and ordered them ashore---a pilot who happened to be on board, we retained and with the promise that his life should be spared on the condition that he would carry us in safety to the south of the line—terms which, as his life was at stake, he did not hesitate to accede to, and after reaching a particular latitude, and selecting one from among our number as captain or chief of our gang, we delayed not in commencing operations—giving chase to and capturing everything of inferior or equal force that we could meet with, without respect to nations.

On the 13th February, near the island of Ascension, we fell in with an English ship, the *Morning Star*, Capt. Gibbs, from the island of Ceylon for London, with a full cargo of coffee, and cinnamon, and on board forty or fifty souls, including seventeen sick soldiers, and several women and children.

The savage treatment—nay, the worse than savage treatment, accompanied with acts of unexampled atrocity and enormity, which the poor unfortunate and unoffending creatures (particularly the females) received from us, was such as if ever equaled, could never have been surpassed. Having first ordered the captain with four of his men on board the brig, we proceeded to strip the ship of everything valuable that could be easily removed---this done, the remainder of the men on board, including the sick soldiers, were confined in the hold, and the wretched females and the children being secured in the cabin.

Atrocities Committed on Elderly Women and Mothers As Their Children Watched

We next proceeded to prepare our minds by the free use of the liquor found therein, for the commission of crimes, a bare recital of which is calculated to fill the mind with horror—we proceeded to commit such excesses as decency forbids that I should mention!

What renders it still more shocking to humanity, is the fact that these brutal outrages were committed, among others, on two or three who were very aged, and on some who were mothers, and in presence of their children!

God of Heaven! I would exclaim, can it be possible that I, not then exceeding twenty-five years of age, born

21

of, and brought up under the admonition and pious examples of respected parents, could have been the subject of so sudden a transition from principles of virtue and innocence, to those of vice and infamy, as to have willingly participated, and with a degree of diabolical satisfaction, in such atrocious and wanton acts of cruelty and outrage!

Horrid as it may appear, it was even so, yes, true it is, that by our habitual use of spirituous liquors, my mind was rendered no longer susceptible of a single tender feeling, but had become obdurate, debased, hardened and depraved, and prepared for the commission of any crime within the catalogue of human depravity!

The Wicked Never Go Unpunished

Providence who never suffers the wicked to go unpunished, has now numbered my days, and is prepared to cut me off in all the bloom of my sin, and wickedness, and exhibit a signal example of merited punishment.

After feeling no longer a disposition wickedly to indulge ourselves in excesses the most shameful and diabolical, we felt not unwilling to destroy the lives of those miserable and unfortunate beings, who had been made the wretched subjects of them!

Together with that of their still more wretched offspring!—with the women and children still confined to the cabin, and the men (including the sick soldiers) to the hold, without a possibility of their being able to liberate themselves, the ship was by us scuttled and abandoned, and soon after sunk to the bottom with, every soul on board!

To close *the* tragic scene, the captain and four men whom we had retained on board the brig, were next, murdered and their bodies thrown into the sea!

We Murdered 25 Souls an Hour

Thus, in the short period of two hours, from the time that we got possession of the ill-fated ship, between forty and fifty innocent and unoffending fellow beings, (male and female) were without provocation precipitated in the most awful manner from time into eternity—when but a few hours previous, were not only thoughtless as regarded personal danger, but probably elated with the prospects of a short and prosperous voyage, and anticipating the pleasing reception they should meet with from relatives and friends when arrived at their destined port!

Alas, fools must we all have been, to suppose that such an act of unexampled atrocity could go unpunished!

Nay, it cannot, and I feel that my career of guilt and wickedness is now drawing to an end—it has reached a climax of horror, of which history does not probably afford a more remarkable instance of human depravity.

I cannot but hope that my dreadful example will be held up as a beacon to others, who may be in a course of vice and drunkenness that they may avoid the rock on which I have been irrecoverably wrecked.

Looting & Burning of *Topaz*,
Murder of All Hands

A few days after the capture and destruction of the English ship, we fell in with a richly laden American ship (the *Topaz*) bound from Calcutta to Boston, to the crew of which no more mercy was shown than to that of the *Morning Star*.

Having laden our brig with a portion of the most valuable part of her cargo, the crew (with the exception of the captain and three hands, who were taken on

23

board the brig) were all put to death, and the ship set on fire!,

In a few days after, the captain and two of the three hands shared the fate of their companions.

We had now indeed from repeated instances, become so familiarized with the shedding of human blood that the shrieks and groans of the devoted victims were but music to our ears!

And the work of human butchery was performed as deliberately and; with as much unconcern as the butcher, would, dispatch one of the brute animals of his flock!

Soon after the capture of the Boston ship, it was concluded by a majority on board most advisable for our own personal safety, to steer for Azores, and from thence to some port in Spain, there to dispose of the brig and the property on board, plundered from the captured vessels.

And after sharing to each an equal portion of the proceeds, to separate and each one to seek new quarters and new business for himself.

This being finally concluded upon, we set sail accordingly, and on the passage fell in with and plundered four ships with valuable cargoes, among which was the Portuguese ship *Malinda*, by some of the crew of which we were unfortunately recognized as the same who belonged to the brig, which had lain near them in the Rio de Janeiro.

This was the first instance in which a single one of us had been recognized by the crew of any of the captured ships, as persons they had ever seen before.

We had a short and safe passage to Pontevedra, and from thence soon after sailed for Coruna, where we arrived in the latter part of April.

Dead Men Tell No Tales

On the passage there being still some suspicious persons on board, and some among our own gang, it was thought best by a majority on board to dispatch them, and thus put it out of their power to betray us

Accordingly four of the suspected who had been our ship companions, and the last surviving victim of the Topaz (whose life until now had been spared) were put to death. The manner in which one of the former (*Caravallo*) suffered, is sufficient to satisfy those unacquainted with the fact, with what deliberation and seeming indifference life could be taken—and even that of one who until now had been viewed as a true and faithful companion!

Bloodthirsty Song of Praise for Our Leader

Teto (one of the three who volunteered to perform the deed) shot at and wounded him in the head, and then stabbed him in the stomach, Babazain and Antonio (two others selected for the purpose) gave him each severe stabs in the body, and while in the agonies of death, the latter caught him in his arms and threw him into the sea.

Then staining his hands with his blood, and in proof of the satisfaction he had taken in performing the deed, commenced in singing a song in praise of Benito, our chief.

Pursued by Spanish and Captured

Having thus accomplished our object in destroying the lives of every suspicious person on board, by whom we thought there could be a possibility of being through treachery betrayed, and after sharing equally of the plundered property in our possession, those who preferred it went fearlessly on shore, and separated—

25

while others preferred remaining on board the brig-, and to engage in another cruise—but this proved an unwise choice, for some who had left her being suspected, apprehended and closely examined, disclosed the whole, and the brig and all on board were soon after captured by a Spanish government cruiser sent in pursuit of her.

Some who landed were so fortunate as to make their escape, but the prospect is great of their all being soon taken, as great rewards it is said are offered for their apprehension by the Spanish and Portuguese governments—and Benito (our chief) I am informed is already taken and is now in close confinement in Gibraltar, awaiting the punishment which he merits, and which the violated law of nations demand.

Sentence of death has been passed upon myself and nine others and tomorrow is the day appointed on which we are to be made an ignominious example of!

**We showed no mercy,
none should be shown for us**

When I take a retrospective view of the many horrid crimes of which I have been guilty—-of the many innocent victims whom, in concert with others, I have deprived of life, in the course of the last five preceding years, I cannot but acknowledge the justness of the sentence.

And believe it consistent with the laws of God, and for the welfare and safety of mankind, that we should be made a public example of—for, having shown neither mercy nor compassion to our fellow-creatures, we have none to expect from the hand of man!

And O, what a warning ought it to be to all, who while young, unwisely indulge themselves in the immoderate use of ardent spirits!

Had this not been my first fault, I might now, in all probability- so far from being under sentence of death, as a wretch unworthy to live, and doomed with bands yet crimsoned with innocent blood, to suffer with nine others an ignominious death on the gallows, have been esteemed as a respectable member of society, and an honor *to* and the support of my neglected parents, in their declining years of life--but, alas, the die is cast.

The irrevocable sentence of death, which fixes my doom, has been pronounced!

It is impossible for anyone to have a true conception of the horrors of mind which I now suffer—being sensible that I have, as I have been charged, repeatedly assisted in perpetrating the horrid crime of murder, and under circumstances of greater aggravation, of more cool premeditated atrocity, than it has ever before probably fallen to the lot of man to see or hear of!

The Demon Rum

Parents into whose hands this my dying declaration may fall, will perceive that *I* date the commencement of my departure from the paths of rectitude and virtue, from the moment when I became addicted to the habitual use of ardent spirits.

—and it is my sincere prayer that if they they val*ue* the happiness of their children—if they desire their welfare here, and their eternal well-being hereafter, that they -early teach them the fatal consequences of Intemperance!

NICHOLAS FERNANDEZ

SENTENCES AND EXECUTION.

After the legal process, and the hearing of the defense of the criminals, the tribunal before which they were tried, condemned them to suffer the punishments respectively as in the following form. Banitt Soto, to be hung, dragged along the ground and quartered, and the quarters placed on hooks on the sea shore.

Jose de los Santos to be hung quartered, and his head placed on a hook on the sea shore—that a description of his person be sent to the authorities of the marine, to the Peninsola and West Indies, in. order that he should be sent back to Cadiz for execution.

Nicholas Fernandez, Antonio de Lagoa, Saint Cyr Barbazan, Maria Guillermo Toto, Frederico Lerenda and Nuno Pereyra, to be hung, quartered and their heads to be placed on books on the sea shore.

Francisco Goubin, Pedro Antonio, Doming Antonio and Joaquin Francisco to be hung.

The Pilot, **Manuel Antonio Rodriguez** to 10 years in the house of Correction and to be present at the execution.

Cayetano Ferreira to 8 years in the House of Correction, to be present at the execution.

Manuel Jose de Freites to 6 years in the house of Correction from the time he has been in prison and to be present at the execution.

José Antonio Silva and Antonio Joaquin to six years imprisonment without the above deduction and to be present at the execution.

The Negro slave **Joaquin Palabra** to be present at the execution and to be given up to the Portuguese Consul to be sent to his owner. The whole in conformity to the laws.

The several sentences of death were executed in front of the bay in Cadiz on the 29th of December last.

The measure of their crimes was now filled, and Divine Justice was, regarding them, to put an end to their crimes, and to make them suffer punishment in the very country in which they wished to enjoy tranquilly those riches which, we may say, were still smoking with human blood. Discovered and made prisoners, by one of those accidents, the foresight of which is not in man's capacity, and in which the hand of Providence is manifest, they have suffered that punishment of which they were so deserving.

The memory of the atrocious deeds which they committed, the innocent blood which they spilt, and the many persons who were the victims of their ferocity, would excite general indignation, and all will applaud the wise disposition of the authorities, who, satisfying public vengeance, have freed society of some monsters who could not but continue to fill it with evils and terrors of the most direful kind.

***

Of the ten Pirates executed on the 29th December, pursuant to their sentence, the nativity and parentage of the unfortunate **FERNANDEZ** (then but 26 years of age) is fully related in the preceding pages—of him we shall add no more than to say, that of the whole ten, he seemed to die the most penitent—he acknowledged the justness of his sentence, and seemed to entertain a proper sense of the enormity of his offences, and to the very last moment continued to warn those by whom he was surrounded to beware of that most odious and destructive vice—INTEMPERANCE. He was the only one of the ten that appeared to have been well educated, but by unfortunately yielding to the arts and persuasions of bad men, he early contracted a habit of intemperance which appears soon to have destroyed whatever there had been of liberal humanity in the bosom of the ill-fated youth.

ANTONIO DE LAGOA, reported himself (after condemnation) to be by birth a Portuguese, and of wealthy and respectable parentage, and apparently of about 30 years of age—he declined making any confessions more than that previous to entering on. Board of the Brazilian brig, he bore an unimpeachable character, but lost it by associating with bad company, and that as he had now by his bad conduct not only brought himself to a shameful end, but destroyed forever the peace and happiness of his once beloved parents, he should decline accepting a pardon if offered—it was his wish to die!

BARBAZE and TETO, were both (as represented by themselves) Frenchmen, born in the south of France, and in appearance and naturally, the most hardened and consummate wretches that ever disgraced human nature.

They were equally addicted to habits of excessive drinking, when under its baneful influence their ferocity was excited to that degree that their thirst for human blood appeared almost insatiable!

It seemed to fit them for the commission of any crime, and the more innocent and defenseless the victim, the more pleased and gratified they appeared in the sacrifice—and while on board, were frequently heard to boast of having "shed as much innocent blood as would float the brig!"

Their age and immediate place of nativity, as well as particulars relative to their former adventures, are

30

unknown, as they declined disclosing anything relative thereto, either while in confinement or at the place of execution—when the fatal hatters were placed upon their necks, and were informed that they had but a very few minutes to live, they seemed in no way moved or effected thereby, but to the last exhibited the strongest symptoms of impenitence and unrelenting hardihood!

LERUNDU and PEREYRA were both Portuguese and both natives of Oporto, the former was 32 and the latter 37 years of age—like **BABBAZEN and TETO** they exhibited no proofs of penitence, but seemed rather to relent that they were so be deprived of an opportunity of adding to their bloody catalogue of murdered victims, such of their late companions as had treacherously betrayed them—at the place of execution they appeared like savage monsters rendered desperate by their crimes, and too familiarized with death to feel much intimidated at its approach.

They even in the la-t moment of their existence were heard to reproach the unfortunate **FERNANDEZ** for exhibiting tokens of penitence and for expressing fears of a still greater punishment in the world to come.

FRANCISCO GOUBIN, PEDRO ANTONIO, DOMINGO ANTONIO and JOAQUIN FRANCISCO-. were all Brazilians, and three of them under the age of thirty.

They were sentenced only to be hung, as they were thought in a degree less- culpable than the others, they having composed a part of the brig's original crew, became the dupes of older offenders. By the aid of liquor and with assurances that no more would be required of them than to hold their peace and remain quiet spectators of the massacre of such of their shipmates as it would be found necessary to put to death!

These unfortunate and deluded young men unaccustomed to witness such shocking scenes of human butchery, as they were afterward compelled to witness, would have relented and voluntarily made a full disclosure thereof to proper authority, had not their more artful companions (when such opportunities offered)-taken the precaution to prevail on them to drink to that degree as to render them, incapable of such disclosures.

They were all four much addicted to the intemperate use of liquor, and although its introduction in prison after the condemnation of the prisoners, was strictly forbidden by the police, yet notwithstanding three of the latter were evidently so much under its operation in the last awful moment of their earthly existence, as to be launched almost in a state of stupid insensibility into eternity!

FATAL EFFECTS OF INTEMPERANCE

As the reader must be satisfied by the dying declaration of the unfortunate **FERNANDEZ**, as well as by what is stated relative to such of his wretched companions in their last moments, who very justly suffered with him, for their heinous offences, that the awful and ignominious punishment to which they were doomed, for the perpetration of crimes of a most barbarous nature, may in a very great degree be attributed to affixed habits of excessive drinking.

Part Two

Pirates or Privateers?

The is the story of the capture of a merchant ship by Confederate pirates after she left port in New York City in 1863 during the height of the U. S. Civil War. The story is told in reports from newspapers in Nova Scotia, New York and London and in the official records of the trial of those who seized the ship in the name of the Confederate States of America in a trial held in Canada.

This chapter deals with the story of the piracy of the steamer Chesapeake on Dec. 5th, 1863. Was this an official and legally sanctioned act of a privateer acting against U.S. shipping and authorized by the Confederate States of America?

News reports of the "Daring Act of Piracy" are included here along with the actual trial of those charged with piracy.

In addition to the unusual and intriguing story of the seizure of the steamship Chesapeake is that the act of the United States gunboats entering territory of the British North American colonies and seizing the ship, thereby violating the sovereignty and neutrality of Britain, combined with another act, came close to bringing England into a state of war with the United

States, and France declaring it would join England in such an effort.

CAPTURE OF THE STEAMER
CHESAPEAKE

Harpers Weekly
NEW YORK, SATURDAY, DECEMBER 26, 1863.

ON Wednesday, December 9, H. B. Cromwell Co., of this city, received a telegraphic dispatch from the Mayor of Portland stating that the steamer *Chesapeake*, owned by them, had been captured twenty miles north-northeast from Cape Cod, at half past one o'clock, Monday morning, by British pirates, who had started from New York as passengers. The *Chesapeake*, of which we publish a sketch on this page, was on her way to Portland, Maine.

From statements made by Captain Willett, who commanded the steamer, we learn that the piratical party consisted of fifteen persons, headed by a Mr. Osborne, a coast pilot from St. John, New Brunswick. The whole party concerned in the perpetration of this daring outrage—an outrage which did not stop short of cold-

35

blooded murder—was made up of British subjects, residents of St. John and Carleton, New Brunswick. The seizure took place in the following manner:

The Captain had retired for the night. The second engineer (Owen Shaffer) had charge of the engine, and the chief mate (Charles Johnson) held the watch.

At a quarter past one the pirates were up and doing. The first notification of their presence was given in the deliberate and unnecessary murder of Shaffer, who had just returned from oiling the engine when he received a mortal wound in the neck. Johnson, the mate, was going to the pantry, and witnessed the deed. On his way to the captain's room he was himself fired at, and received two wounds, one in the arm and another in the knee.

He succeeded in arousing the captain, who, soon after his arrival on deck, was put in irons, having been fired at fifteen or twenty times, but, strange to say, without injury.

The chief engineer (James Johnson) also was wounded.

In all these cases of firing at the officers of the *Chesapeake* there was no attempt at parley, no warning of any sort: the pirates were sheer cowards.

The officers being all secured—one of them killed, two wounded, and the others put in irons—the helmsman and third engineer alone being left at their posts, Osborne took charge of the vessel, and all was quiet again. After the seizure the prisoners were treated with great consideration, and the bona fide passengers, five in number, were left at their liberty, on condition of their non- interference. These five passengers were all old sea-captains. All the ordinary operations usual on shipboard went on as usual until Tuesday morning, when the vessel was brought to anchor in Seal Harbor, off the island of Grand Manan.

Thence she was brought up the bay toward St. John, having received on board a new captain, viz., John Parker, of the privateer Retribution. At Dipper Harbor, twelve miles from St. John, the captives were allowed just ten minutes to transfer themselves and their baggage to the pilot-boat, which was towed up to within seven miles of St. John by the *Chesapeake*, when the latter cast off tow and returned down the bay, picking up on the way a schooner supposed to have had guns, ammunition, coal, etc., on board for the new pirate.

These pirates gave Captain Willett a copy of "Orders from the Confederate Government," which is without official seal—a mere fabrication, which will not save the rogues from hanging if they are caught. Similar plots, it is believed, have been formed against other vessels. The Chesapeake was built in 1852, by J. A. Westervelt, and is 460 tons burden.

(Author's Note: This news report from Harper's Weekly incorrectly reported that the pirates in question were British. They were predominately Confederates, although one of them was a British subject.)

The U. S. Gunboat Ella & Annie recaptured the Chesapeake

Capture and Recapture of the *Chesapeake*

The Illustrated London News, vol. 44, no. 1239, p. 34. January 9, 1864

The *Chesapeake*, Captain Willet, screw-steamer, of 460 tons, one of a line of freight and passenger steamers sailing between New York and Portland, Maine, left New York on the 5th ult., on her regular trip to Portland. At one o'clock a.m. on the 6th of December, 1863, when about twenty miles N.N.E. of Cape Cod, she was seized by a party of Confederates, who had taken passage on her for Portland. The second engineer, who was in charge of the engine at the time, was shot dead and his body thrown overboard. The first engineer was wounded by a ball in the chin, and was kept on board to work the engine. The first mate was also wounded, but not dangerously; and although several shots were fired at the captain he was fortunate enough to escape without even getting a wound.

After the crew had been overpowered, the vessel was taken charge of by the Confederates; the captain, officers, and crew were placed in irons, and the passengers, some six or eight in number, on promising not to interfere, were allowed their liberty. The Confederates numbered sixteen persons, and were commanded by a Lieutenant Braine, reputed to hold a commission in the Confederate service.

Among the passengers was a man belonging to St. John, New Brunswick., who, on its being ascertained that he was acquainted with the navigation of the Bay of Fundy, was forced by Braine to act as pilot. On the night of the 8th the *Chesapeake* arrived off Musquash Harbor, where she was boarded by a person, said to be a Confederate officer, who assumed the command of the steamer.

A passing pilot-boat, "*The Simonds*," was hailed, the pilot was compelled to come on board, and the boat was taken in tow. The passengers, captain, officers, and crew of the *Chesapeake* were landed at this place, and arrived at St. John, New Brunswick, on the morning of the 9th of December.

This incident forms the subject of our Illustration on the preceding page, from a sketch by Mr. Charles C. Ward, of St. John. The *Chesapeake* then steamed up to Partridge Island, at the mouth of the Harbor of St. John, where the man who had acted as pilot was landed, and the vessel sailed away.

The *Chesapeake* has been subsequently recaptured by the Federal steamer Ella Annie, in Sambro Harbor, Nova Scotia. The *Chesapeake* was taken to Halifax for judicial decision. No resistance was offered by the crew, all of whom, except three, escaped to the shore. The English authorities in Nova Scotia had forbidden the furnishing of coals to the *Chesapeake* by the people of that province; they had ordered her detention wherever she appeared, and gave the information to the Federals which led to her capture. It is also alleged that they have ordered the arrest of the men who seized her while going in her as passengers, holding them to have been guilty of piracy.

We learn by the last mail that the three pirates captured on board the *Chesapeake* were taken from the authorities by the mob whilst being landed at Halifax, and set free.

THE CAPTURE OF THE *CHESAPEAKE*
The Piracy Conceived at St. John, N.B.
FULL EXPLANATION OF THE PLOT.
A Party of the Vilest "Roughs" Concerned in it.
The Steamer in Harbor Near Cape Sable.
Further Concerning the Chesapeake.
The Navy and the Captured Steamer *Chesapeake*.
ST. JOHN, N.B., Thursday, Dec. 10.

The ***Evening Globe*** gives the following connected with the capture of the *Chesapeake:*

The scheme was matured here by Confederate agents. Meetings were held, and the passage money of parties to make the seizure was paid through to New-York. They were promised $500 each on the steamer's being safely taken into Wilmington. It was also arranged that at a certain store in New-York each of the parties was to call at different times for a parcel containing a revolver, ammunition and a pair of handcuffs. It is believed that the cargo was shipped by Confederate agents was valuable to the South, and that it was arranged that she should be seized on this particular trip.

The manager of the plot represented that the *Chesapeake* had been taken while attempting to run the blockade and this was a harmless effort to get back Southern property. We have the names of five of the parties engaged in the seizure. They belong to this City and left here with Capt. BRAINE. They are of the worst species of humanity denominated "roughs." One of them was just out the penitentiary.

They all went from here by the steamer New-England on the 3rd to Boston. The *Chesapeake* did not coal here. She called off the harbor, and took on board Capt. PARKER, formerly of the privateer *Retribution*, who took command. The citizens generally regret that this city has unwittingly afforded temporary shelter to the concoctors of the scheme, and that any person from this place should be concerned in it. Public opinion condemns the act entirely. Capt. MILLET and the passengers and crew were provided for by the steamer New-England to-day.

LATEST -- The *Chesapeake* is reported to be below Publican harbor, near Cape Sable.

It is stated by the owners of the captured steamer *Chesapeake*, that there is little probability of the pirates now in charge of her taking the vessel into Wilmington, N.C., as she was not built for that trade, and could not be got up the river. It is possible; however, her captors may attempt to shelter the steamer under Fort Castle, one of the fortifications in the hands of the rebels on Smith's

Island, about forty miles below Wilmington. Should they do this, it would only be with a view to discharge the cargo and burn the vessel; for to get her out to sea again from that point would be next to impossible, as her whereabouts could not be concealed from the blockading fleet. It is now known the *Chesapeake* did not leave St. Johns until after 4 o'clock Wednesday morning, and it is thought probable she will waylay some steamer, "coal up," and endeavor to reach some free-trade port.

If this program is pursued there is but little doubt of her capture, as prompt measures have been taken, detailed in our naval news, to, overhaul her. The Captain and crew of the *Chesapeake* probably arrived at Portland yesterday. They are expected in this City to-day when full particulars can be obtained. The *Chesapeake* is of the same size and nearly the same model of the *Sumter*, but is a much stronger and faster vessel. Should the pirates succeed in escaping the vigilance of our gunboats and properly arm her, she will prove a formidable foe to our commerce.

Oil Painting of the Seized Ship Brought to Navy Yard to Instruct Naval Officers to Aid in Search!

On receipt of the information that the steamer *Chesapeake* was captured by a band of rebel passengers, Admiral PAULDING telegraphed a statement of the case to the Secretary of the Navy. The dispatch had hardly been received when Mr. WELLES telegraphed back to the Admiral to select a fleet of the fastest vessels at the yard, to charter some others, if thought necessary, and send them after the captured vessel. All day yesterday the yard swarmed with naval officers, coming to tender their services for the chase. The owners of the *Chesapeake* were also at the yard, and conveyed over an oil-painting of their vessel, which was inspected by all the officers about to search for her.

Fleet Assembled With All Due Haste to Scour the Seas for the *Chesapeake*

About noon the Admiral selected the splendid steamer *Grand Gulf*, the new steam propeller *Vicksburg,* recently purchased, with a fleet of vessels from the Neptune steamship Company, the United States steam gunboat *Sebago*, and the chartered steamer *Potomac*, which resembles the *Chesapeake*. The vessels had hardly received orders to prepare for sea, than the Navy-yard presented a scene of the most unusual activity. Sea-stores, provisions, and all other necessaries were hurried on board with the greatest dispatch; officers and sailors hastily picked up all their necessary luggage and got themselves ready for a cruise. The vessels which were short-handed received additions of men from the receiving-ship *North Carolina*, a portion of whose sailors were also sent on board the *Potomac*.

The latter vessel also received a pretty formidable armament -- one which will enable her to give a good account of the prize if she sees her. It is stated also that orders have been sent from the Navy Department to Philadelphia and Boston, ordering the commanding officers of those naval stations to send away immediately, such vessels as are ready at the yards commanded by them.

Another rumor says that the *Sassacus*, one of the fastest ships in the navy, which recently made seventeen miles an hour on her way to Washington, was sent away from the National capital this morning to search for the *Chesapeake*. The *Sassacus* is commanded by Commander

KEN ROSSIGNOL

ROE, who was recently the Ordnance Officer at this station.

At 3 o'clock, everything being ready for sea on the vessels named, the following fleet left the harbor: United States steamer *Grand Gulf* (new) with the following list of officers: Commander, J.M. RANSOM; Lieutenant, Frederick Bragon; Acting Ensigns, C.J. Frijole, John Boyle, H.J. Ipsom, C.B. Cachen; Surgeon, G.B. Higginbotham; Paymaster, E.B. Southworth; Engineers, C. McEwen, S.V. Shelbring, J.M. Wheeler, F.O. Reynolds, Benj. James, Geo. W. Shuertt; Master's Mates, Mason, Courtney and Cleaves. The steam gunboat Sebago with the following list of officers: Lieutenant-Commanding, J.E. DEHAVEN; Acting Masters, W.H.V. Millard and Jerome B. Rogers; Assistant-Acting Surgeon, Titus M. Coan; Assistant-Paymaster, H.A. Strong; Acting Ensigns, Chas. B. Dorrance, E.D. Martin, S.G. Blood; Assistant Master's Mates, R. France, W.C. Peel; Assistant Gunner, J. Roberts; Acting First Assistant Engineer, F.A.R. George; Second Assistant Engineer, W.P. Ayres; Acting Third Assistant Engineers, R. Miller, B. Kelley, F. Ballard.

The United States steamer *USS Vicksburg*, with the following list of officer: Commander, D.S. Browne; Assistant-Acting Surgeon, T.W. Bennett; Assistant Acting Paymaster, T.E. Smith; Acting Master, Jas. H. Rodgers; Assistant Ensigns, J.H. Harris, F.G. Osborn, W.H. Bryant; Assistant Master's Mate, A. Vanderbilt; Second Assistant Engineers, W.C.M. Durnbryne, H.H. Dellers, F. Blark Dorsen.

Lieut. HOEY, of the Navy, was designated to command the *Potomac*, which vessel, we believe, also went away late last evening. It was reported late in the evening at the Navy-yard that the *Dawn*, the prize-steamer *Peterhoff*, and other vessels, were ordered to depart; but they had not left the Navy-yard at 5 o'clock,

44

and there was apparently no work going on with them. Another account of the proceedings at the Navy-yard and station, sent to the naval reporter, stated that Admiral GREGORY, superintendent of iron-clads and double-enders -- not connected with Admiral PAULDING's department -- had received instructions to dispatch seven or eight of his double-enders to sea. But this rumor, also, turned out to be untrue.

Rumors and Hoaxes Embellish the Piracy of the *Chesapeake*

We believe that the commanding officers of the vessels which left last evening had instructions, in case they met other fast steamers of the navy cruising, to request their commanders to search for the *Chesapeake*.

All sorts of rumors were current during the evening about the proposed action of the Department. One of them was to the effect that the Mayor of Portland had requested Secretary WELLES to send to that city all the steamers he had at his command which could not be manned, and men could be found in Portland to fill up their crews. But this was evidently a hoax, as no dispatches were received, up to a late hour, ordering any vessels to the city named. A private dispatch, received here last night from Philadelphia, states that the new steamer *Kansas*, recently built for the navy there, is also ordered to sea.

DARING ACT OF PIRACY
The Steamer Chesapeake Seized
by Rebel Passengers
Crewman Shot Dead and Thrown Overboard
Crew and passengers put ashore at St. Johns, N.B.
Officers wounded, Captain put in irons
Pirates Put to Sea, Fleet sent in hot pursuit

The New York Times
Published: December 10, 1863
ST. JOHN, N.B., Wednesday, Dec. 9.

The steamer *Chesapeake*, (owned by H.B. CROMWELL Co.,) Capt. WILLETT, from New-York for Portland, Me., was taken possession of on Sunday morning last, between 1 and 2 o'clock, by sixteen Confederate passengers.

The Second Engineer of the steamer was shot dead and his body thrown overboard.

The First Engineer was shot in the chin, but was retained on board.

The First Mate was badly wounded in the groin.

Eleven or twelve shots were fired at the Captain.

After being overpowered, the Captain was put in irons, and the passengers were notified that they were prisoners of war to the Confederate States of America.

The steamer came to off Partridge Island at about 1 o'clock this morning.

The crew and passengers, except the First Engineer, were put on board a boat and sent to this city.

The steamer then sailed in an easterly direction, and was subsequently seen alongside another vessel. It is supposed that she took on board a supply of coal from her.

The attack took place about twenty-one miles west of Cape Cod.

Capt. WILLETT and passengers per the Chesapeake are now at the Mansion House.

The following telegraphic dispatch was received by Mr. CROMWELL this morning:

PORTLAND, Wednesday, Dec. 9.

H.B. Cromwell & Co.:

Steamer *Chesapeake* was captured twenty miles N.N.E. off Cape Cod at 1:30 A.M. on Monday morning by rebels who left New-York as passengers Second Engineer killed and thrown overboard. Chief Engineer and Mate wounded.

Capt. WILLETTS and crew were landed at St. John this morning.

The *Chesapeake* carried a crew consisting of Captain, two mates, two engineers, two coal passers, four men before the mast, cook and steward. The capture was made during the hour of midnight, and but one watch was on deck, and but two men in the engine-room.

The Captain had retired, and thus, while they were quietly sleeping, was this outrage committed. The Second Engineer, Mr. ORRIN SHAFFER, undoubtedly had charge of the engine, and in all probability met his fate through his bravery. He has been a long time in the employ of this line, and has always won the respect and esteem of his employers. He was a young man, and leaves a wife and children. The Chief Engineer, JAMES

47

JOHNSON, and Chief Mate, CHAS, JOHNSON, both of this City, were wounded.

Seven passengers obtained their tickets at the office, and among them was one person who stated to the clerk that he was an old sea Captain, and preferred this mode of reaching Portland on account of its being the pleasantest and cheapest. Before she started some fifteen persons were counted on her deck, and as it is usual in this line for persons to sail without having purchased their tickets, nothing was thought of this circumstance. She left full of freight, consisting of cotton, rags, provisions and general merchandise. She only carries about thirty tons of coal, which is enough to last her for the round trip, and had not more than three days' coal at the time of her capture, so that the rebels cannot get very far with her. She carried two guns, 6-pounders, one brass the ether iron, several revolvers, and some other fire-arms.

It is not known whether there was any powder on board, but it is supposed there was not much. Her sails were small and cannot be depended upon. There was no war risk, and the value of the vessel is over $60,000. It is not known whether the cargo was insured. The Captain is expected to arrive here to-day, and then the full particulars will be obtained.

The steam propeller *Chesapeake* was owned by H.B. CROMWELL, of this City, and was a splendid vessel in every respect. She was built in 1853 by J.A. WESTERVELT -- was 460 tons burden, and 11 feet draft of water, built of oak, schooner rigged, and had a direct acting engine of 200-horse power; one cylinder of 40 inches and 42-inch piston. Her ordinary speed was from 10 to 11 knots, but she could be driven at the rate of 14 miles per hour. She has always been a propeller boat on this route, and was the vessel which chased Capt. REDD, of the *Tacony*, at

48

the time of his famous foray in Portland Harbor, June 27, and succeeded in capturing his vessel, the schooner Archer.

The following is a list of the officers of the *Chesapeake:* Captain, I. Willett; First Officer, Chas. Johnson; Second Officer, Daniel Hendon; Third Officer, John Anderson; Chief Engineer, James Johnson; Second Engineer, Owen Shaffer (killed;) Third Engineer, A. Scrubby; Steward, Patrick Kelly; Stewardess, Jennie Bergoin.

The steamer *Potomac*, which was to have sailed yesterday for Portland, was detained.

PORTLAND, Me., Wednesday, Dec. 9 -- 10 P.M.

Deputy-Collector BIRD has applied to the Washington authorities for permission to dispatch, the Agawam, the new gunboat now furnishing hereafter the *Chesapeake*, and in the meantime the Collector is fitting her out with guns, men and provisions. Two detachments of soldiers have been furnished for the expedition by Brigadier-Gen. ROWLEY from the conscript camp, and Major ANDREWS from Fort Preble. She will sail about 6 o'clock this evening, under command of Capt. WEBSTER, of the revenue cutter *Dobbin*. Citizens are volunteering as crew.

PORTLAND, Me., Wednesday, Dec. 9.

A private dispatch received this evening says there are many suspicious characters about St. Johns, and there are hints of a plot against the steamer New-England.

Permission has arrived to put the gunboat Agawam in commission, which Deputy Collector BIRD had already taken the responsibility of doing.

The United States Consul telegraphs that it is thought that the Chesapeake had proceeded to Halifax. We are indebted to the Consul for all previous dispatches about her.

BOSTON, Wednesday, Dec. 9.

The United States gunboat Acacia left here this evening to search, for the steamer *Chesapeake*.

The name of the commander of the pirates who took the *Chesapeake* is HENRY BRAINE. Lieut. BARR one of MORGAN's men, is second in command. They said they would attempt to run into Wilmington.

Crowd Aids in Escape of Pirate
The British Colonist

Accordingly, the *Chesapeake* was delivered over to Captain O'Brien; and a boat arrived from the *Ella and Anna* with the three men.

They were marched up the slip closely guarded and handcuffed, in which condition the High Sheriff refused to receive them, when the irons were removed by the officer in charge, and the Sheriff, after reading the necessary documents pronounced the men free.

Immediately following this proceeding a scene occurred, which, as it is the subject of a good deal of comment, and caused a great deal of excitement, we shall describe particularly.

During the proceedings, no one gave any attention to a boat which tossed about in the chop at the slip, in which sat two men who might have been attracted to the spot from the fish-market slip just opposite. The moment the Sheriff pronounced the men free, a gentleman who had placed himself during the reading of the documents, close beside Wade, told the latter to jump into the boat, and before anybody could realize what was going on the boat was two or three lengths of herself from the wharf.

At this instant a policeman dashed through the crowd and shouted to the men in the boat to stop or he would shoot them dead, at the same time drawing a pistol from his pocket.

Two or three gentlemen interfered and obstructed the policeman, and the boat, with Wade in it, escaped.

The New York Times
THE *CHESAPEAKE.*
Published: March 5, 1864

The following novel notice appears in the Richmond papers:

EASTERN DISTRICT OF VIRGINIA, SS.:

The President of the Confederate States of America to the Marshal of the Eastern District of Virginia.

Greeting:

Whereas, a libel has been filed in the District Court of the Confederate States of America for the Eastern District of Virginia by P.H. AYLETT, the District-Attorney of the said district, in behalf of said Confederate States, against the steamer *Chesapeake*, a vessel belonging to the United States of America, her tackle, apparel, furniture and cargo, for the reasons and causes in said libel aforesaid mentioned, and alleging and propounding that, since the commencement of the existing war between the United States of America and the said Confederate States, to wit:

On the 8th day of December, 1863, JOHN C. BRAINE and HENRY A. PARR, citizens of, and enlisted in the service of, said Confederate States, and JOHN PARKER, an officer connected with the schooner *Retribution*, a vessel belonging to the said Confederate States, provided with a letter-of-marque, issued by the Department of State of said Confederate States, as well as divers other citizens of the Confederate States, under command of the parties aforesaid, did capture at sea the said steamer *Chesapeake*; and further alleging and propounding that said steamer Chesapeake is now lying in the neutral harbor of Halifax, in Nova Scotia, within the dominions of Her Majesty the Queen of Great Britain, and praying for the usual process of monition of the said court, and that all persons interested in the said steamer, her tackle, apparel, furniture or cargo, may be cited to answer the premises; and, all proceedings being had, that the said steamer, her tackle, apparel, furniture and cargo may, for the causes in said libel mentioned, be condemned as lawful prize of war: you are, therefore, hereby required and commanded to cite, and give due notice to, all persons claiming the same, or knowing or having anything to say, why the said steamer, her tackle, and so forth, should not be condemned, pursuant to the prayer of said libel, by causing a copy of this monition to be published in the *Richmond Sentinel, Enquirer and Examiner,* four times in each of the said newspapers, at least fourteen days before the day of appearance and return day of this process hereinafter mentioned, that they be and appear before the said court, to be held in the city of Richmond, in the said district, on the 22d day of March next, at 12 o'clock, noon, if that shall be a day of jurisdiction; otherwise on the next day of jurisdiction thereafter; then and there to interpose a claim for the same and to make their allegation in that behalf; and have you then and there this writ, with your return thereon.

Witness.

Honorable Judge JAMES D. HALYBURTON. Judge of the District Court aforesaid, the 23d day of February, 1864.

LOFTIN N. ELLETT, Clerk.

The Trial

THE *CHESAPEAKE*

THE CASE OF DAVID COLLINS, ET AL,
PRISONERS ARRESTED UNDER THE PROVISIONS OF THE
IMPERIAL ACT, 6 & 7 VIC, CAP. 76,
ON A CHARGE OF PIRACY,
INVESTIGATED BEFORE
Humphrey T. GILBERT, ESQ.,
POLICE MAGISTRATE
OF THE CITY OF SAINT JOHN,
THE ARGUMENTS ON THE RETURN TO THE ORDER
OF HABEAS CORPUS,
HIS HONOR, MR. JUSTICE RITCHIE,
HIS DECISION
COMPILED FROM THE ORIGINAL DOCUMENTS.
SAINT JOHN, N B.,
.I. & A. MCMILLAN, PUBLISHERS,
PRINCE WILLIAM STREET, 1864.

THE importance and peculiar circumstances of this case have induced the publishers to present to the public all the proceedings taken before the Police Magistrate, and also before His Honor Mr. Justice Ritchie, with the evidence in full, and the various documents on which the arrest was made, together with those produced in evidence on the investigation.

Every effort has been used to publish a correct report, and the publishers in the compilation, have had the assistance of Charles W. Weldon, Esq., one of the Counsel engaged, and of William M. Jarvis, Esq., the reporter to the Law Society of Decisions at Chambers.

As this is the first case which has arisen in New Brunswick under the Treaty of Extradition of 1842, and the object and nature of the tenth article of the Treaty, with the mode of procedure thereunder is so fully discussed, and other questions of international law presented that the publishers believe that the publication will be of interest to the people not only of this Province, but also to those of the neighboring Colonies, and the United States.

KEN ROSSIGNOL

THE *CHESAPEAKE*
DAVID COLLINS, ET AL.

Shortly after the retaking of the *Chesapeake* in Sambro, Nova Scotia, some of the original captors having returned to this Province, the United States Consul in St. John addressed to the Hon. S. L. Tilley, the Provincial Secretary, and two letters under date 22d Dec, 1863.

Accompanying these letters was an affidavit jointly made by Isaac Willett, Captain, and Daniel Henderson, second mate of the steamer, detailing the facts within their knowledge concerning the capture of the steamer; the said affidavit having been sworn to before H. T. Gilbert, Esq., Police Magistrate and a Justice of the Peace for the City and County of Saint John, on the twenty-second day of December, A. D., 1863.

On these papers His Excellency the Lieutenant Governor issued a warrant under the provisions of the Act of Parliament 6 and 7 Vic, cap. 76.

Mr. Gilbert, on receiving His Excellency's warrant took the complaints of Captain Isaac Willett, and on the 25th day of December issued his warrant to apprehend certain persons therein named, and upon which warrant David Collins, James McKinney, and Linus Seely, parties named therein were arrested and brought before Mr. Gilbert for examination on January 4th, 1864.

Andrew E. Wetmore, Esq., Q. C, and William H. Tuck, Esq., appeared for the prosecution on behalf of the Federal authorities.

Hon. John H. Gray, Q. C, and Charles W. Weldon, Esq., appeared for the prisoners on behalf of the Confederate States.

56

PRELIMINARY EXAMINATION.

Before the examination commenced Mr. Gray asked Mr. Wetmore to elect upon which charge he would now proceed, and to state in whose name he was proceeding. Mr. Wetmore replied that he would only state that he was proceeding upon the complaint of Isaac Willett. He first stated that he would take up the charge of murder, and subsequently decided to proceed with that of piracy, in the first instance.

Mr. Gray then objected: Says Court Has No Jurisdiction Over Piracy

1. That this Court has no power or jurisdiction to try for the offence of Piracy. That for the trial of Piracy a Special Commission must issue and a Court be specially constituted for the purpose; and that such Court is distinctly provided for by the Imperial Act.

2. That the Warrant was insufficient. It does not show upon the face facts which are essential, under the Treaty with the United States, to bring this matter into the Courts of this Province, or to create the special jurisdiction, which enables us to arrest parties under those charges. [Mr. Gray cited the case of Dillan, charged with an offence on the sea beyond Provincial jurisdiction that was arraigned before Judge Parker at the last circuit, and discharged. And Mr. Weldon cited the case of the brig Eliza, in 1847.]

3. Not only is the Warrant insufficient on these grounds but on the face of it is bad, as charging two distinct offences triable before two different tribunals. There ought to be two Warrants.

Mr. Gray thought these objections fatal to any proceedings.

Mr. Wetmore replied at some length, and read a large portion of the Provincial Act passed to give effect to the Extradition Treaty. He claimed that everything so far was regular, and that the Magistrate could not go back of the warrant, which was sufficient authority for him.

The Magistrate told Mr. Gray that there was probably something in his argument; but that at present he would proceed with the preliminary examination, and if he decided before the case was through that he had no jurisdiction he would give the prisoners the benefit of it.

The following Witnesses were then examined:

EVIDENCE OF CAPTAIN WILLETT.

Captain Isaac Willett sworn:

"I am a citizen of the United States—live in Brooklyn—a seaman for 30 years—know the *Chesapeake,* owned by H. B. Cromwell, also a citizen of U. S.—was master of her in December, and had been for 17 months—she was re-built in New York about 3 years ago—previous to that she was called the *Totten"*

[Mr. Wetmore asked where she was registered? Both Messrs. Gray and Weldon objected to the question as improper. The Magistrate agreed with them.]

"During the 17 months the vessel plied between New York and Portland—she had a coasting license."

[Mr. Gray objected to any evidence respecting contents of this license; objection sustained.]

He had the paper until it was taken away from him on board the ship.

"On the 4th and 5th Dec. I had charge of the *Chesapeake,* then lying in North River taking in cargo for Portland. Most of the freight was taken in on the 5th, Saturday. She carried passengers also. I saw these three prisoners on board on the trip in question."

"Saw them first about supper time, about six o'clock in the evening. We left New York on the .5th December; I was in the wheel house when the vessel left the wharf. They did not buy tickets, paid their money on board. I identify Collins and recognize the others. I wrote their names on a piece of paper and gave it to a Stewardess to arrange rooms for them."

[Wetmore asked the names of the other persons on board. Gray objected; objection over-ruled.]

"There was a person who called himself John C. Braine, said he was Colonel. Understood there was a person named Brooks—don't recollect the names of Seely and Clifford. All the passengers paid their passage except two. We proceed direct to Portland from New York; do not call. The vessel, a propeller, was worth $60,000 to $70,000. There was an assorted cargo, flour, sugar, wine, and such like. Do not recollect the owners— do not know its value—probably $80,000 to $100,000."

A MIDNIGHT MURDER –ATTEMPT ON CAPTAIN'S LIFE AS WELL

"There was no disturbance until Monday morning, 7th. We were then about 50 miles N. N. E. of Cape Cod. Cape Cod is in the United States. About a quarter past one in the morning, the first thing I knew, the Chief Mate, Charles Johnston came to my room and called me saying somebody had shot the second Engineer, Orin Shaffer."

"I turned out of my room and went to see how badly he was shot, and had hardly time to get out of my room before I was shot at. I was at the engine room door, on the upper deck where my room was. I found the body of the second Engineer lying on the deck; it is more than I could tell whether he was alive or dead; he appeared to be dead. I was in the act of stooping down to raise him up, when I was shot at twice."

CAPTAIN TAKEN PRISONER IN NAME OF SOUTHERN CONFEDERACY

"I then walked forward and was shot at again. I supposed to be from a pistol; next day I saw two places in the deck where pistol balls had gone through right by where I was. I can't tell who shot at me. I only saw two persons then. I cannot identify either of these prisoners as the parties. I saw no marks of violence on the Engineer, but I saw marks of blood where his head lay. When I walked forward I was going into the pilot house, when I was collared and a pistol was put to my face by first Lieut. H. A. Parr, who was in the pilot house. He collared me and said I was his prisoner in the name of the Southern Confederacy."

"Parr put the irons on me—two or three others stood beside him. They seemed to be standing there doing nothing. He put handcuffs on each wrist. The irons could be made small or large. They put me into my own room; I could have come out when I pleased. No use for them to lock the door. I don't know what became of the body of the Second Engineer, except what I heard from the others. I was confined an hour, when Parr and sailing master Robinson came to me. They didn't say much, but took me into the cabin—there I saw some of the other passengers who were not concerned in the affair. While I was there the chief mate Charles Johnston and Chief Engineer James Johnson were brought in wounded; I had heard reports of fire arms."

Captain Observed Pistol Wounds, Removal of Leaden Ball from Mate's Arm, Engineer's Chin

"The mate was wounded in the right knee and left arm. The wounds appeared to be made by pistol shots. I saw the leaden ball taken out of the mate's arm. He suffered considerably from the knee, not so much from the arm. Lieut. Parr took the hall out of the arm. The chief engineer was wounded by a ball in the hollow of the chin. Parr said he would get the balls out of them if he could, and fix the wounds. The chief mate laid on a lounge until he was put on board of the Pilot Boat. I remained in the after cabin until 8 am the next morning."

"The irons were then taken off and Robinson went up to my room on deck with me; I was in the room a few minutes and returned to the cabin. When on deck I saw Collins and Seely there; Seely was scrubbing brass on one of the timber heads; the others did not appear to be doing anything in particular."

"Ship was taken from me by these parties against my will and consent"

"Col. John C. Braine took my ship's papers from me in the afternoon before I was landed in the Pilot Boat. Braine seemed to have command of the vessel; she was taken from me by these parties, against my will and consent. I saw Mr. McKinney on board the vessel. They seemed to be about the vessel and appeared to be eating the grub up as fast as possible. Don't recollect of seeing McKinney doing anything. The person who was navigating the vessel was named Robert Osburne, a passenger, one of the six who bought tickets in New York. None of the parties named in the warrant had tickets. The first land we made after they took possession was Mount Desert. I asked them where they were going, they said Grand Manan; I asked where they intended to land me, they said St. John. Mount Desert is on the American coast east of Portland. I would not see it if I were prosecuting a voyage from New York to Portland.

61

After passing Mount Desert we saw land east of that place. We proceeded to Seal Cove Harbor, Grand Manan. The boat was lowered, three or four men went ashore, remained a little while and came on board again, when the steamer left and came up the bay to St. John."

Ship's papers seized by Confederate Pirates

"Next I was taken up to my room by Braine and Parr; Parr made a copy of Braine's instructions and Braine gave it to me. He ordered me to give up the coasting license, and permits for the cargo, and the money I had collected from Braine for his party, in all §87. He asked for the money he had paid over to me ; it was my employer's money ; I knew it would be worse for me if I did not ; I handed it over against my will ; Braine had a pistol in his hand at the time; I handed money, ship's papers and permits to him. The papers were the ship's coasting license from the New York Custom House, under which she was coasting at the time, as required under the American law. After this they (Braine and Parr) took me away from the room, took me aft and ordered me to stay there. We then saw a pilot boat. We were on our way to St. John."

The Plot Thickens as New Captain Comes Aboard

"The pilot boat ordered us to stop; someone came on board the steamer from her, stayed a few minutes and returned. Then Captain John Parker came on board and apparently took command. They then took the pilot boat in tow and steamed up to Dipper Harbor. All of the passengers and crew, except two engineers (James Johnston and Auguste Striebeck) and three firemen (Patrick Connor was one,) were put on board the Pilot Boat. The firemen and engineers were kept against their will. Those who went on board the Pilot Boat were myself, Charles Johnson, the chief mate, Daniel Henderson, three boys and four sailors, whose names I
62

do not recollect, the stewardess and five passengers. One of the passengers belongs some thirty miles back of St. John the other four belonged to Maine. These five passengers had tickets. Robert Osburne remained on board the *Chesapeake;* he also had a ticket. The steamer towed the boat some five or seven miles and let go of us; we were put on board the boat about five in the evening; that was the last we saw of the steamer."

"I landed in St. John about four on Wednesday morning; I got a boat from a big ship near Partridge Island and came to town with four of my men and two passengers. From the way the parties acted in my steamer I was afraid of my life. Everything was taken against my will. I saw one or two of these prisoners on watch; they were on deck. I supposed they were on watch. They seemed to be acting as other men would who were on watch. Braine's party assisted him in charge of the vessel."

"As far as I know these men were assisting him. I did not see them making sail, or shoveling coal. I don't recollect of seeing Collins or McKinney doing anything, except being on deck."

Cross-examined by Mr. Gray:

"I don't deny there has been war in my country for two or three years between those calling themselves Confederate states and the United States."

[Mr. Wetmore objected to this as an improper way of proving a state of war. The Magistrate did not think this evidence could be shut out.]

"I can't remember how many States are called the Confederate States—Virginia, North Carolina, South Carolina, Georgia, Alabama, Mississippi, (about-one-third of the latter). Abraham Lincoln is President of the United States, and Jeff. Davis is President of the Confederate States. I never heard of Mr. Benjamin, Confederate Secretary of War. I have heard they say they have a Government.

I have read Lincoln's Proclamation of war against the South, ordering them to destroy the property of the South, but I do not recollect its contents. I never took notice of it to ..."

[Here the witness was stopped.]

"...Parr *did* put a pistol to my head in the pilot house and said he took me prisoner in the name of the Southern Confederacy. They put the irons on me rather hard. They did not say anything about taking the vessel in the name of the Confederate States then. After they took the handcuffs off there was always a guard with me when I went about. I did not see any act of violence towards the passengers after the capture of the vessel. The handcuffs were also removed from the officers. I left a copy of the 'instructions,' which Braine left with me, in New York."

Mr. Gray asked the Captain the substance of these instructions;

Mr. Wetmore objected.

Mr. Gray argued the point, and then read from a manuscript a copy of Capt. Parker's order to Braine, (which Captain Willett had published in the *New York Herald* and other papers), and asked the Captain if the copy was correct.

The witness said it was nearly correct. The name of the Sailing Master in the copy handed him by Braine was George Robinson, not Tom Sayers; the name of the Engineer was not given in it, and the number of the men stated was 11, not 22. In other respects Mr. Gray's copy was correct.

Captain's Arsenal Seized by Confederates

"The Confederates kept of my private property, one double barreled gun, one single barreled, 5 five barreled revolvers, and 1 six barreled revolver, I did not come out of my room in what they call my shirt tail. They kept me aft and plundered my room. They took 3 coats. I missed them when I commenced to pack up. I brought ashore my clock, 8 charts, sextant, and 3 books. The passengers also brought ashore their own things. I did not see Braine give the passengers money to take them back to New York. The crew brought part of their things ashore."

"They put us into the Pilot Boat six or seven miles this side of Dipper Harbor. I did not see and do not know that the Confederate flag was raised over the vessel."

Pirates Fired Two Shots at Captain and Missed, 'Must Have Been Bad Shots'

"They fired two shots at me, and I don't know how many more. The first two shots were fired at twelve feet. They must have been bad shots. The *Chesapeake* had two six-pounders forward, and of ammunition half a keg of powder. No cutlasses. The Confederates who cut out the *Caleb Cushing* at Portland were sent to Fort Warren; I have heard so. The *Chesapeake* was engaged in retaking the *Caleb Cushing*. I saw the Confederates who were then taken they were sent to Fort Preble. I do not know that those Confederates were ever trial as pirates or in any other way. Only Lieut. Parr told us that their party was acting for the Confederate Slates. They all seemed to be working together, and were working under Parr and Braine. I was not at Sambro, and did not see the steamer after I got into the Pilot Boat. None of my crew to my knowledge was kept in irons the next day—the day after

KEN ROSSIGNOL

the capture. I never saw or heard of Braine or Parr before.
Re-examined by Mr. Wetmore:
"I have heard the Confederates called rebels in the Northern States generally. The *Caleb Cushing* was lying at a wharf in Portland Harbor when captured. Braine was called 'Colonel'; the parties all seemed to be working together. I cannot tell whether Braine paid the passage of these three men, the prisoners.

JANUARY 6, 1864.
EVIDENCE OF DANIEL HENDERSON.
Daniel Henderson, sworn:

"I reside in Portland, Me.; I am second mate of the *Chesapeake* in the beginning of December. Five or six years ago I was employed on board her, and had been for two or three years. She was called the *Chesapeake* then, and traded from New York to Savannah, Charleston and Baltimore, and sometimes to Portland. She had previously been called the *Totten*, but when she was rebuilt her name was changed. She was owned in New York by H. B. Cromwell."

"She was latterly employed in the trade between New York and Portland. She lay in North River, New York, at Pier 9, on Dec. 4th and .5th, and took in considerable cargo. She had a great deal of wine and cotton, and was nearly full. She left on Saturday 5th, about 4 in the afternoon. She had 22 Passengers. This was not an unusually large number. She sometimes had 50, or 60, or 70."

"The crew numbered all told—including the stewardess—18. I paid no particular attention to the passengers, and the only one I knew was Braine, who had been a passenger from New York to Portland about a fortnight before, and then had a wife and child with him.

He then said he had just come from England. The voyage usually occupied 36 to 37 hours."

"On Sunday night at twelve o'clock my watch was over and I went to bed. My room was on deck immediately adjoining the pilot house. I had not been in bed more than an hour and a half when four men came to my door, broke the lower panel, and then opened the door. This awoke me. The four men then stood holding pistols over me—pointed at me—and bade me get up and put on my clothes. I did so. They then ordered me to put my hands together and hold them up, and they put handcuffs or irons on me. They told me when doing this that I was a prisoner to the Confederate States. I asked them if I could not see the Captain or someone belonging to the vessel. They told me, "I couldn't see nobody". They then locked me in my room. About ten minutes after I heard a noise as if of a man falling on the deck near the pilot house door, and I then forced the door of my room open. The deck was covered with ice and I slipped and fell and then two of those other fellows caught me by the shoulders and hauled me into the pilot house, where I sat in a corner."

Second Engineer Killed
and Thrown Overboard

"About 20 minutes after, Braine came in and said that the second engineer had been killed and thrown overboard. Several of those fellows went in and out of the pilot house while I was there. The prisoner Seely, who seemed to be keeping watch forward, went in twice to warm himself. A big tall fellow, with a long sandy beard, was steering. Neither of the other prisoners went in. He stayed some time there. One of the other fellows an officer came to me and asked me where the paint was; I told him in the paint lockers. The officer then ordered me to show him where it was, and I went down and showed him."

Ship Name to Be Covered with Paint

"The officer said they wanted to paint out the steamer's name, and the yellow streak on the funnel. The officer held a pistol in his hand. I asked him to have the irons removed, but the officer refused. They were not taken off until the next morning about 7 o'clock. I was taken to the passenger cabin and found the mate there wounded in the right leg and left arm lying on a mattress, and the engineer wounded in the chin, and others of the crew and passengers. I asked Braine to allow me to sit by the mate and attend him. Braine said he would see what could be done and sometime after told me I could sit with the mate and I did so and washed his wounds. A man armed with a revolver sat by them, and another also armed, kept guard at the cabin door. The prisoner McKinney was at one time on guard and was armed. When breakfast was ready they were taken to breakfast. "

Armed Guards at Breakfast Table

"Two men armed with revolvers stood on each side of the breakfast table, and McKinney, armed, stood on the stairs outside. I went on deck two or three times during the day, having obtained permission to do so. No guard accompanied me, but armed men kept guard on both sides of the steamer. Collins was one of the men on guard, and held a pistol in his hand. I saw Seely cleaning some brass work on the timber head. I was kept close prisoner all day, and pretty well down. At night they were all ordered below, the officers were put in the cabin and the rest of the crew in the forecastle, except the firemen who they kept at work. About six o'clock one of

68

the officers, with a pistol in his hand, came down to the cabin, and ordered me to go up and show them how the bells from the pilot house to the engine room were worked. I did so, and then asked where all our men were, and the officer told me they were down in the forecastle."

"Next morning they made Grand Manan. Braine came down to the cabin and ordered me go up and get ready the anchor to let go when they wanted to. This was, I understood, at the suggestion of the man who belonged to the other passengers, and not to those fellows, but who was acting as pilot for them."

Ordered to drop anchor at gunpoint

"Braine, with a pistol in his hand, and the other man stood over me while I prepared the anchor. They reached a harbor and the anchor was let go. They then had breakfast. I did not eat much. I was too uneasy, as I did not know what was to become of me. I could not get any of them to tell me, and I did not know but I might have to go over the rail. After breakfast they lowered a boat and Braine and two or three of his men, as well as I could see through the cabin windows, went ashore. They remained two or three hours, then returned and weighed anchor. Sometime afterwards, they met a pilot boat. The boat ordered the steamer to stop, and a man came on board the steamer from the boat, stayed some time, then went back to the boat, and soon after he and another man came on board the steamer and brought a valise."

"I was kept aft on deck at the time and could see what went on, but could **not** hear what was said. The man went forward to the pilot house, could not tell what his name was, or whether he took command. This was two or three hours after they left Grand Manan. The steamer then proceeded towards Saint John, having the pilot boat in tow. Sometime after, all of our crew was put on board the pilot boat except the two engineers and three firemen, who were kept on board the steamer, and five of the passengers were also put on board. The other passengers who had acted as pilots remained on the steamer."

Passengers set adrift three miles from shore

"The five passengers who were put in the boat had been taken prisoners like the others. The steamer towed them to within about 3 miles of Partridge Island, and then let them go and kept right on. It was about 8 o'clock when the steamer left the boat. We stayed in the pilot boat until 10 o'clock next morning, when they were brought to the steamer New England. Capt. Willett, with some of the crew, and all of the passengers, got a boat from a ship and came up to Saint John about 4 o'clock in the morning."

Liner Paint Markings Masked by Black Paint

"I was in bodily fear from the time the vessel was taken from us and our crew until I got out of the pilot boat. I am not in the habit of being afraid under ordinary circumstances. The prisoners were on board the steamer when the pilot boat was cast off, and went off in the steamer; they had no place to land. Some of the parties got a stage over the stern, for the purpose of painting out the name of the steamer, and they said afterwards that they did so. They made our men paint the yellow streaks on the smoke pipe black. The *Chesapeake* carried the Stars and Stripes—the American flag. I never knew of her sailing anywhere except to American ports, and from one American port to another. The captain and crew had no control over her, or cargo, after she was taken possession of on Monday morning."

70

"The second engineer might possibly get the apparatus for throwing hot water without help, but I doubt if he could, at all events he could not do it in less than twenty-five minutes. He would have first to go on deck from his engine room, then uncoil the hose from the hose box and extend it along the deck, then attach it to the goose neck on deck, then take it down to the engine room and put the machinery in motion and after that return on deck to use the hose."

Mr. Gray said all this was immaterial, as if a man under such circumstances as would create the impression that he had the means of throwing hot water immediately threatened to do so, the effect would be precisely the same as if he actually had the means of carrying out such threat.

The witness also said I heard Braine and the Chief Engineer disputing as to whether the Second Engineer had fired a pistol shot.—Braine said he must have fired the first shot. The engineer denied that he had fired, and said he would lay any wager that he could then, if Braine would let him make the search, find that pistol (it is presumed the pistol Shaffer owned) in the Second Engineer's room in his bed. I heard afterwards that it was found. I saw blood on the place where they told me Shaffer had fallen. Shaffer was nearly six feet high and a stout able man. He was a very kind, gentlemanly man, and very much liked by the whole crew. He was about 45 years of age, and I often heard him say he was born up North River, in the State of New York.

The only names I remember having heard were those of Braine, Parr, and Collins. All the party seemed to be acting under Braine's command.

Cross-examined by Mr. Gray. — "From the time the vessel was taken until I left the pilot boat I was in bodily fear. I have not told more than occurred. A great many things happened that I did not see in coming to Saint John by train I did not get out at a way station, for fear of coming to Saint John. I came the whole way in the train. When the vessel was seized and they told me I was a prisoner to the Confederate Stales, I knew what they meant."

Ship Did Not Fly Stars & Bars

"I did not see the Confederate flag run up. I do not know that the North has taken many Southern ships; they may have taken some, but I do not know how many. I did not see the order given to the captain by Braine; heard something about it. The captain told me they had given him their names, but did not tell me they had given him a copy of the order. I was not treated with any unkindness, but the engineer was kept on duty after being wounded, and bleeding from the chin. I was allowed to take all my clothes when leaving the vessel. The cotton we had on board came from New York. I could not say whether it came from the Southern States or from Europe. Cotton is one of the chief productions of the Southern States."

"I have known cotton to come from Europe. No one was hurt who did not make any resistance to the capture. I did not hear Braine say that he gave orders to his men not to injure any one, unless in case of resistance. On Monday morning after they had secured possession of the vessel, all of our men, that I could see were liberated from the irons. One of Braine's men told me that if I would keep quiet, and not attempt to recapture the vessel, they would take care of me. I believe the passengers got all their luggage. I lost nothing, and am not aware that any of the others lost anything, except what the captain spoke of."

Re-examined.—"They told me they were acting in the name of the Confederate States. The chief engineer was forced to work after being wounded in the chin. I do not know what became of the second engineer's luggage. I did not know he was killed, as I was asleep at the time."

January 8, 1864.

EVIDENCE OF JAMES JOHNSTON.

James Johnston deposed — "I was born in Ireland; have been a resident of the United States 14 years; am not a naturalized citizen of the United States ; follow the business of engineer; know the steamer *Chesapeake;* was Chief Engineer of the steamer *Chesapeake;* have been Chief Engineer something over *a* year; have been on board the steamer *Chesapeake* three years last July; was on board the *Chesapeake* on the 4th and 5th December last; this vessel was engaged in carrying passengers and freight between New York and Portland; the steamer had something over twenty passengers on board on the 5th December; I had charge of the engine on the 5th ; remained in charge up to 12 o'clock at night ; nothing unusual occurred on Saturday night or on Sunday; I had charge of the engine again on Sunday night until 12 o'clock ; was waked up between 1 and 3 o'clock on Monday morning by the report of pistols; went from my room on deck and found Mr. Shaffer lying on deck at the engine room door."

Second Engineer Was Dead; I Was Shot

"I knew the steamer 14 years ago; she was then called the *Chesapeake; have* known her by the name of the *Totten; she* was at one time rebuilt; she was rebuilt in

New York; she was afterwards called the *Chesapeake*; I had known her by the name of the *Chesapeake* before that time; she is owned by H. B. Cromwell, of N. Y. I raised the second engineer up when I found him lying on deck on the Monday morning of the capture; I called him by name; he was dead and lying with his feet down the hatchways ; this was between 1 and 2 o'clock ; I saw no blood then, it was quite dark; saw two spots on his neck which showed blood; I then went below to the place from which the second engineer came up; there I got a pistol put to my head by Collins; I caught him by the arm, and told him to hold on, then a man beside Collins whom I took to be Brooks, shot at me, the ball taking effect in the chin.

[**Mr. Gray** objected to witness answering the question "who shot the second engineer?" Brooks made a statement; it appears, to the witness with reference to the shooting of the second engineer, which Mr. Gray objecting, the magistrate would not allow him to tell as not being admissible in evidence.]

Saw Mr. Shaffer's body going overboard

"I went across the deck below and spoke to Wade. Wade did not answer. I was fired at without a word being said to me. I had the ball taken out of my chin two days ago. It was taken out by Dr. Earle of King's County. The mate Charles Johnston was shot in the knee and in the arm. He and I went into the kitchen through a little hatch; we remained there for half an hour. While there I saw Mr. Shaffer's body going overboard. There were three or four persons engaged in throwing it over. I knew none of them except Braine. The body was thrown over just as it was when lying on deck. The cook came to the kitchen. I asked him where Capt. Willett was. He said he was in the Cabin. I also asked him what was going on. He said the ship was taken."

74

"Robinson, the sailing master, took me to my room to dress, as I had only my night clothes on. I had been asleep and was awakened by the pistol shot. Robinson had no pistol with him that I saw. I heard two or three pistol shots."

Captain Kept in Irons

"After dressing I went to the cabin and found the Captain there in irons; Robinson was with him; the mate was there wounded; Parr was there taking a shot out of Brook's hand, he then took a shot out of the mate's arm ; Parr then tried to take the shot out of my chin, but could not, as he said it was fast in the chin; I do not remember to have seen any of these prisoners present; I had some conversation with Parr; who told me to keep the cold out of the cut; he assisted me in wrapping it up; we had no conversation in reference to the firing of the pistol. I spoke to Capt. Willett; I went with Robinson to the engine room to see if all was right there; there was nobody there but Striebeck, the oiler or assistant; I went there against my choice."

The Captain asked me if the ship was safe

"Capt. Willett asked me if the ship was safe, I told him she was not, and Robinson overhearing my answer, got permission of somebody to take me there, and see if there was any danger of the ship blowing up, as Striebeck was not an engineer and had been on board the ship but a short time. I did not remain there long; I went back to the cabin after telling the oiler how much steam to carry. After being in the cabin an hour, I went back to the engine room. There was someone with me all the time, a guard I mean; I was taken back on the second time to attend to the engine, and see if the engine was all right. I was then acting for Mr. Braine; Braine said he had no engineer, and that I would have to act. I was not in a fit state to work, on account of the wound in my chin, which was bleeding. I had to be at the engine all the time, as I had no assistance, there was someone on guard all this time. The prisoners were among those who were on guard; those on guard were armed with revolvers. I was not threatened. Two by the name of Cox, and two by the name of Moore, Treadwell, Wade, and the three prisoners, also Lieut. Parr and Brooks, were among those on guard over me, the guard was changed at stated times."

Braine was brains of the plotters

"Braine had command of these men, these are all the names that I can remember, these men acted under the orders of Braine, Parr, and the sailing master. As far as I could see, Robinson was the sailing master; he was in the engine room pretty much all the time."

"I slept on the locker in the engine room. I was not on deck much; did not see much that was going on, on deck. The vessel did not stop till she reached Grand Manan. She remained there two or three hours; after leaving Grand Manan we sailed towards St. John, and got below St. John harbor about 7 or 8 o'clock on Tuesday evening; we remained at anchor."

"We stopped before reaching St. John, and got Parker on board from a pilot boat; he took charge over Braine; there was another gentleman, Mr. McDonald, came on board with Parker; he was introduced to me by Parr as Mr. McDonald; Mr. McDonald told me to content myself for a little while, as he would only keep me for 48 hours; he appeared to be concerned in the affair. "

"I told him I wished to get home as my folks would be uneasy ; he asked for my address, and he said he would send a dispatch to my wife, and inform her that I was well and would be treated well; he forgot his kind intentions, however, as the dispatch was not sent. McDonald went ashore here. I saw .McDonald a few days ago. He came from Halifax to the Bend with me, I did not request him to come, and perhaps he came to see that I got through safely."

"We remained off Partridge Island in the steamer from three to five hours; a boat went ashore, in which were Parker and Braine. I do not know any of the others, or what they went ashore for. They came back to the ship and we started as soon as we could get steam up after they came aboard. I think McKinney went ashore with them. We did not take in any coal here, we left here about 2 o'clock next morning under steam, and we got into Shelburne in the first place, got there about 9 o'clock on Thursday night."

Chesapeake steamed to Shelburne in heavy gale and snow

"Capt. Parker had charge of the vessel on the way to Shelburne, I was not allowed to go ashore, neither was any of the crew. There were four others of our crew taken away in the vessel; their names were Striebeck, Connors, Tracy, and Murphy. I had charge of the engine, I slept at little at one time, and I slept three hours in the cabin. We had a very heavy gale of wind, also snow on the passage, which commenced on Thursday morning. We lay at anchor in the harbor; we lay there all Thursday night. We took in coal and wool there from a schooner on Thursday night. Parker told me there were ten tons of coal, and two cords of wood."

"Here we discharged a large quantity of freight, including flour, sugar, and tobacco and port wine. It was

77

put on hoard a schooner. I do not know how much wine was put ashore. The wine was put up in quarter pipes. The wine was distributed about the vessel. I got some. Capt. Parker said that Kenney, a man living there, had bought a thousand dollars' worth of the cargo. Braine came back there in the day time; I cannot say on what day. We lay there 4 or 5 days. We were there on Sunday. Do not know on what day we sailed. Braine left the vessel again while there. He took a trunk with him; I heard there was jewelry in it Braine did not come back there again. Got no additional men or coals at LaHave. We got some wood. Parr told me that he was going away for a day or two. He would return and bring Braine back, when he would endeavor to get the captain to liberate me, as it was too bad to keep me confined to the ship, wounded as I was and away from my family."

Parr also said Braine had acted wrong in running off with a sum of $400.

(Mr. Gray objected to all evidence as to some statements made by Parr, and quoted from Roscoe's evidence in support of his objections. The Magistrate ruled in his favour.)

Witness resumed: — "Parr went away. I do not know where. We left that evening. I do not know the date. We got some wood there. We left La Have and came to the mouth of the river, towing a schooner of about 50 tons, and loaded with part of the cargo of the *Chesapeake.* I cannot say what kind of a load we gave her as it was at night, but it was a pretty good load. I did not hear Parker say what he got for this; we got some wood from the schooner. We remained at the mouth of the river and then proceeded to Sambro, about 20 miles from Halifax. Our coals lasted until we got there. We got no additional crew at La Have. Capt. Parker went from Sambro to Halifax for coal, but took no part of the cargo with him. He returned with a schooner load of coal, two engineers, and two firemen. Parr had not returned. We commenced taking in the coal about 2 o'clock in the morning. I got up and spoke to Parker. He told me about the men he had got, and asked me to show the engineers the machinery. I told him I would after daylight."

Gunboat appears, pirates flee *Chesapeake*

"After that I was in my stateroom gelling ready to leave, Parker having told me he was done with me, when the pilot (Flynn) reported to Parker that there was a gunboat in the harbor. Parker went on deck, and seeing her spoke to his new engineer about getting steam on. (This place they call Mud Cove.)"

"The engineer told Parker his men were not in order to get steam on. Parker then told me to scuttle the ship but I told him I did not know how. He said I could cut a pipe, and I said we had no pipes that I could cut. Parker left the cabin then. I carried my clothes on deck, and found him and his crew leaving the vessel and very good time they made. The three prisoners were among them."

"I then got an American color out of the wheel house, and one of the firemen to run it up Union down. The gunboat came alongside and boarded us. She was commanded by Lieut. Nichols. There were none on board the *Chesapeake* then but myself and my three firemen, the two new engineers who were left behind, and one oil-man. There was no steam up then. Nichols asked me who was on board, and I told him. We tried to get up steam, but we had not coal enough, and no oil on board."

"About an hour and a half after this we left, and proceeded to Halifax in company with the Ella and Annie.

The *Dacotah* was behind us. I stayed in Halifax until Monday last. Parker, Braine and Parr had charge of the *Chesapeake* from the time she was captured until they left her at Sambro. Capt. Willett and his crew had no control over her. I did not act of my own free will, but under orders from these people. I went to the second engineer's room in company with Parr and Striebeck, and found a pistol there which I handed to Parr. He examined it and said it had not been used. In the second engineer's drawer I found the pistol.

"The second engineer's room was on the deck above where he attended the engine, and the same deck on which I found him dead. I hired him about two years ago, and have never known him to carry a pistol. I would have known it if he had done so. There was no means of putting boiling water on deck, nor were there at any time. There was a force pump to throw cold water in case of fire. I saw these prisoners every day from the time the vessel was captured until they left her at Sambro. They all carried revolvers. I do not know what position Collins occupied."

Cross-examined by Mr. Weldon.

After being shot, I escaped down dumbwaiter

"When Brooks got to the cabin he was wounded in the left hand. Parr cut the ball out. I heard nothing said about the engineer shooting him. I found the second engineer dead at the top of the gangway, his duty was below. I went down and saw Brooks, who flashed a pistol within about two feet of me. The ball struck me in the hollow of the chin; did not knock any teeth out; but was bedded in the bone. I had it taken out the day before yesterday from the outside. After being shot, I went into the kitchen through a hatch used as a dumb-waiter. This may have been cowardly, but I could not help it. I

80

remained there about a half an hour, when I was taken to the cabin and Parr cut the wound, but could not get the shot out. He then dressed it, and told *me* to keep the cold out of it. He took the ball out of the mate's arm."

No claims made by pirates to seizing ship for Confederate States

"I did not hear the Confederate States mentioned at all, nor did I hear Braine say to any one that they were acting in the name of the Confederate States."

"They used a Seeesh flag in Shelburne. I cannot describe it; it did not seem right to me. Cannot tell how many colors were in it. I could not describe four weeks from now a "rag" that I had seen today. It was not the Stars and Stripes."

"Parr did not tell me they had taken the *Chesapeake* for the Confederate States; but said that he and Braine had travelled in her about a month before, for the purpose of taking her. He also told me he had been in the Southern army, and was a released prisoner; but did not say what part of the Southern States he came from. He treated me very civilly said Parker had not fulfilled his word, and that he would try and get me away. They did not get any new engineers at Shelburne; they would have to "make them" there. I was allowed to go on deck alone occasionally, and took my meals in the cabin. When the vessel was first taken, Braine told me he had no engineer, and I worked the vessel to Grand Manan. Parker then came on board, told me he would have to keep me a little while, and asked me how much money I wanted. I said not to mind money, I would run the ship if I had to do it"

"I suppose Braine acted under Parker after the latter came on board. There was a guard in the engine room in the fire room and on deck, all the time. Parker said Shelburne was his native place; did not say he had been in the Southern Slates. I had never seen him before. We put into Shelburne, La Have and Sambro, and were about 4 miles inside Sambro and about half a mile from the shore, when the *Ella and Annie* took us. When Parker and his party left they took one boat with them. Wade must have gone on board the schooner, as he was found there by some of the crew of the Ella and Annie. I was left in charge of the *Chesapeake.* The two Halifax engineers and Wade were the only persons taken on board the *Ella and .Annie*. The *Dacotah* lay off the harbor, and after speaking her we proceeded to Halifax, having got orders to that effect from her commander. I was kept only until they got engineers. I did not expect any money nor would I have taken any were it offered.

Re-examined by Mr. Wetmore: — "The watch in the engine room and fire room were armed; I don't know whether the watch on deck was armed."

January 11th, 1864.

Mr. Wetmore put in evidence: Certified copies of the following

Acts of Congress;

Act of Congress 1819, cap. 75,

 Statutes at Large. 3 vol. 514.

do 1820, cap. 113, do id 600.

do 1823, cap. 7. do id 721.

do 1833, cap. 72, do id 789.

do 1825, cap. 87, do 4 vol.

do 1847, cap. 51, do 9 vol. 171.

Also proclamation of President Lincoln dated April 19th, 1861.

EVIDENCE OF CHARLES WATTERS.

Charles Walters was called and testified as follows :— "I reside in Carleton ; have resided there twelve years ; know the prisoners Seely and McKinney ; had no conversation with Seely or McKinney on the subject of the capture of the *Chesapeake;* had heard a good many speak about it in their presence."

Reveals Pirate Plot Hatched in Canada

"I heard their conversation in Lower Cove, in the City of Saint John; McKinney was present. The two Coxes were present; do not know the names of the streets in Lower Cove; do not know in whose house this conversation took place. After going down Charlotte Street, one would turn to the left in order to reach the house in which the conversation took place. it was the next street to the last street which runs east and west; [procuring a plan of the city, the witness pointed out Main street as the one on which the house was situated where these meetings and conversations took place]; the house was on the right side of the street; it was a workshop; it was reached through a yard."

Each Pirate Was To Have Share of Booty

"I saw the Captain there; think his name was Braine; heard conversations there; the Captain was not present; his name was Parker, as I since heard; he was a middling tall man; the captain said he wanted a crew of twenty men to go to New York to capture a vessel. We were all to have a share. I do not know how much each man was to receive; did not hear anything about payment for the service; we were to have our passage paid to New York. Parr was to pay the passage; the prisoners were present at one of the meetings. There were two meetings; I did

83

not hear anybody say they would go; the prisoners were present at the second meeting; there were very few of the boys present at the first meeting; the Captain appointed the second meeting. I never saw Collins before today. I have had no conversation with McKinney about the affair; had no conversation with Seely about it; I won't over to Carleton in the same boat with Seely; I was present when the .American boat went off, and Seely and McKinney were there."

"About a week after the last meeting I heard that the *Chesapeake* was captured; it was asked at the last meeting by the captain if those present would go ; I cannot say that I heard any one assent; I was not present at the first meeting : I saw the prisoners Seely and McKinney the same night that the last meeting took place, before the meeting; I do not know how many meetings were held ; I had a conversation with McKinney and Seely on the road to the meeting, when the prisoners said they would go to the meeting; the two Coxes and a man named George Robinson were with us; Robinson asked the boys to go; they asked where they were going to, and he stated they would find out when they got there ; when I speak of " they " I mean the prisoners and the others ; they asked what they were going for; Robinson said they were going to see Braine, who was holding a meeting for the Captain ; couldn't say what was said on the way ; Robinson called at the Lawrence Hotel and got Capt. Parker and we all went to the place of meeting ; I heard some time before the meeting that this man wanted to get a crew for the purpose of taking a steamer; those who intended to go were to go the next morning; I was present when the American boat left, and saw McKinney and Seely there ; Seely was brought up in Carleton ; I did not intend to go ; I went to the boat to sec who was going ; of those men

84

who were at the meeting [only saw McKinney and Seely; they were on the upper deck of the boat ; did not know where they were going; I bid the time of day to them; I was there about a quarter to 8 o'clock; I left the wharf before the boat left; I heard the steamboat bell ring before I reached the wharf; I was at the head of the wharf when the fastenings were cast off; I saw the prisoners about five minutes before this.

Cross-examined by Mr. Gray.—"It was stated at the meeting by Capt. Parker that they were going on behalf of the Confederate States to take this vessel."

"I think that it was stated at the meeting that this prize was to be divided among the crew by the Confederate Government; Capt. Parker stated that he had a commission from the Confederate Government. The Captain produced a paper which he purported to be a commission from the Confederate Government; the paper was read over; I did not hear what the paper contained; it commenced as near as I can remember - Jefferson Davis, President of the Confederate States of America."

[**Mr. Gray** here produced a document which he refused to allow Mr. Wetmore to see. It was understood, however, that it was the Order of Jefferson Davis to Capt. Parker to go privateering.]

"I think the intention was expressed at the meeting that the vessel was to be taken for the Confederate States, or else they would not have gone; at the time that I heard that Capt. Parker and Lieut. Braine wanted a crew, I also heard that they were officers in the Confederate service."

"I heard at the same time that they wanted to raise this crew for the Confederate service for the purpose of taking this vessel; it was understood that this crew when raised was to be in the Confederate service. I did not hear it said that Parr had been an officer with Gen. Morgan; I was not sufficiently close to see the paper that Capt. Parker read, so as to be able to identify it; I did not see the mark upon it; I was not sufficiently near the paper to sec it so distinctly that if it was now put into my hands I could identify it ; did not sec Braine there the first night ; he was styled Lieutenant ; did not remember that Captain Parker for Capt. Parker, then went down to the place of meeting.

Re-examined by Mr. Wetmore— "I told you all you asked me. The vessel was to be a Confederate prize. I do not know what share we were to have. I think the steamer was to be brought to Grand Manan to land her passengers. There was some talk at the meeting about taking the vessel to Nova Scotia. It was talked among the men that the vessel was to be taken to Nova Scotia. The question was asked if the vessel was to be taken there. I did not hear it asked, and I did not hear the answer. I did not hear what the vessel was going to Nova Scotia for. The men were to have a share. I do not know what they were to have a share of. I can't say that they were to have a share of the vessel and cargo. I did not hear when or where the division was to be made. I did not hear who was to make the division. I heard from Robinson that Parker and Braine were officers in the Confederate service. I did not intend to go with the men. I went to the meetings to see and hear what was going on. It was stated at one of the meetings that the men would be protected.

To Mr. Gray It was stated that the men would be protected by the Confederate Government. It might have been intended that the vessel should go to Nova Scotia for coal.

January 21st, 1864.

Mr. Wetmore put in evidence:—

Certified copy of coasting license granted to the Steamer *Chesapeake*, under certificate of H. Barney, Esq., Collector at New York.

Certified copy of certificate of enrollment of the *Chesapeake* at New York.

The evidence for the prosecution closed.

At the close of the evidence for the prosecution, the depositions were read over to the prisoners and being asked, with the usual caution, what they had to say.

Pirate Says He Was Legitimate Privateer
Collins replied as follows:—

" I am not guilty of any of the charges alleged, and in any and every act done by me, in any way connected with the taking and capture of the *Chesapeake,* I say that act was done under the authority and in the service of the Confederate States of America, Jefferson Davis. President, as I then believed, and now believe. And I utterly deny that I am guilty of piracy, murder, or robbery on the High Seas, or of any crime or offence whatever, and I positively assert that I never contemplated piracy, murder, or robbery, or any other crime or offence, and do not believe I have committed any."

(Signed) D. COLLINS.

The other two prisoners made and signed similar statements.

THURSDAY, 28th January, 1864.

Witness for Pirate Says He Saw Jefferson Davis Letter

The following Witnesses were then called for the defense:

EVIDENCE OF JOHN RING.

John Ring: "I live in Carleton, lived there all my life. I know two of the prisoners, McKinney and Seely. I know Charles Watters. I was present at the meeting spoken of by Watters, about the *Chesapeake;* Watters was there; McKinney and Seely wore there. It was proposed to enter into the Confederate service at that meeting. I saw Braine there, a man they called Braine. I saw a man called the Captain; did not see Parr. I was at both meetings. Some man showed a paper which the Captain said was his authority. I would know that paper if I saw it. I know it by a large seal not quite at the corner; a man's head and shoulders."

"There is another seal on it, on the right hand side, looking like a blot; I minded it when the man read it. I saw it afterwards in Mr. Gray's hands. Jefferson Davis' name was at the bottom of it. I went up and saw what it was he had done reading."

"This is the paper which was produced at the meeting. I swear this is the paper the man read at the meeting. I made a mistake about the head and shoulders of the seal. He had just done reading as I went in. This is the identical paper."

Mr. Gray offers the paper in evidence as part of what took place at the meeting

The Magistrate declines to receive it until it is proved genuine.

Cross-examined.—The seal on the right hand looked like *a* small blot. I cannot say on which side it was, inside or outside.

EVIDENCE OF JAMES TRECARTIN.

James Trecartin: "I live in Carleton. I was present at the last meeting. Ring was there. I think Watters was there. It was proposed to enter into the service of the Confederate States. I was introduced to Captain Parker. I heard a man called Braine was there. I asked the Captain what was his authority, and he pointed to a gentleman and said he will show you my authority, he produced an envelope. He took a paper out, and I saw the red spot on the back. He then read it out. I saw the large seal afterwards on it. It commenced "Jefferson Davis, President of the Confederate States of America. "It was signed on the right hand side"

---Jefferson Davis."

Cross-examined.—It was a round red mark. "Jefferson Davis" was written out in full; there was nothing after it. I saw the paper once at Mr. Gray's; do not recollect the day. I think it was Thursday 7th inst. in the evening. I gave the description of the paper to Mr. Gray, and then he showed me the paper. Mr. Gray and Mr. Weldon were there. I swear this is the paper from the mark shown; the small red seal of the paper. It was a red seal. It was a diamond stamp. I could not say whose name was there."

A certified copy of the commission establishing a Court in the Province of New Brunswick, for the trial of Piracy and other offences committed on the high seas, passed at Westminster the 11th day of April, 1829, by writ of Privy Seal; put in evidence and read.

Asserts War Status of Confederates,
Service in CSS Army
January 30th, 1864.

Certified copies of the letters of the American Consul to Mr. Tilley and affidavit accompanying them put in and read.

EVIDENCE OF LUKE P. BLACKBURN.

Dr. Luke P. Blackburn being sworn said: "I am a resident of the Confederate States. Reside in Natchez, Mississippi. I was appointed Medical Director of the State of Mississippi, in January, 3 1863. I left the Confederate States on 16th July last. I am a native of the State of Kentucky. Have resided in the Southern States since March, 1846, and have been connected with the armies since the difficulty between North and South commenced. I am intimately acquainted with Jefferson Davis, President of the Confederate States. Know his handwriting; have corresponded with him. I know the provisional seal of the Confederate States. A new seal and a new flag were adopted in May last. I'm acquainted with Mr. Benjamin, who in October, 1863, was Secretary of State. The Provisional Government was established in April 1861. Mr. Benjamin acted as Secretary of War for only a short period; he is now Attorney General.

[Mr. Gray here placed in the witness's hand Capt. Parker's authority," and asked him to identify the signatures and seal.]

Witness: "The signature is that of Jefferson Davis, and the Seal is that of the Confederacy. I think that is the signature of Mr. Benjamin. The seat of Government was removed to Richmond in the fall of 1861. A very terrible war is now going on between the United States and the Confederate States."

We Are At War, Prisoners Exchanged

"Prisoners are exchanged. We are recognized as belligerents; sometimes this rule is infringed by the North. I have just arrived from Montreal having left that City last Saturday. Charleston, South Carolina, is in the

Confederate States, and is likely to remain so. The Confederate Government issues Letters of Marque and have vessels of war too. They issued letters of Marque in 1862. The South has a small navy but a very efficient one. I know the South has a vessel of war called the Alabama. In 1862, the States composing the Confederacy were: Texas, Louisiana, Arkansas, Missouri, Kentucky, Tennessee, Mississippi, Alabama, Florida, Georgia, South Carolina, North Carolina, and Virginia.

EVIDENCE OF ALONZO G. COLEMAN.

Alonzo G. Coleman sworn; "I am a resident of the Confederate States and was born and brought up there. I'm a native of Alabama. Previous to the war my father had large estates in Alabama. I have been in the Confederate service since May, 1862. My rank is that of a private. [There was an objection raised to Mr. Gray asking witness whether according to the practice of Confederate service, officers commissioned for any particular duty have not power to delegate authority and appoint others under them to aid in carrying out that duty? The magistrate allowed the answer to be given.]

I have known a Captain to delegate authority to subordinates under him to do a particular act. I have known it to be done.

They have authority to do this. Though a private I have myself been appointed by my Captain to act as Lieutenant to do a particular duty. The acts spoken of were recognized by our commanding officers. I know of such acts being a recognized part of our service. I mean by commanding officers, not Captains but Generals in command. In cases of parties so acting being taken prisoners by the Federal authorities, they are regarded as prisoners of war. The Southern ports are *looked upon* as blockaded. I knew nothing of the *Chesapeake* matter until brought here."

   Cross-examined by Mr. Tuck: "I was not an officer, but was regarded as an officer when placed in command of a party. I only received Private's pay. If a Lieutenant places a Private in command of a party to act for him, he is privileged to act as Lieutenant commanding."

   EVIDENCE OF CAPT. THOMAS HERBERT DAVIS.

   Capt. Thos. Herbert Davis, sworn. "I am a native of Virginia. I'm in Confederate service with the rank of Captain. I went into the service in South Carolina at Fort Moultrie, when the "Star of the West "came up. I went in as a Private, and have gone up through all the grades to a Captain. Have been in active service and have served with Gen. Robert E. Lee's army. Have been with it until within the last six months, during which time I was a prisoner at Johnson's Island. I have served under Johnson, Beauregard and Lee. My division General is Picket. I belong to Longstreet's corps. I have been in every battle except the seven day's battle at Richmond, and the battle of Chancellorsville. I was wounded at Seven Points and was taken prisoner at Gettysburg, and sent to Johnson's Island, from which place I escaped on New-Year's night. That was the coldest night I felt for 12 years. I rode 15 miles, and walked some 120. I borrowed the horses I rode; or rather I took them while the farmers were asleep. According to the practice of our service, officers commissioned to do a particular duly have power to authorize and appoint others to do that duty, or aid in carrying it out; I have exercised it myself. Such acts have always been recognized by my General Officer, and I suppose by the Government) to my knowledge no objection was ever made. It is no novel thing for these appointments to be made. When the persons so

92

appointed to act have been taken prisoners by the Federal authorities, they have been regarded as prisoners of war. I was so treated myself. My Field Officer and two ranking Captains were shot at Gettysburg. After, that until wounded I commanded the Regiment. I was then unable to get off the field, and was taken as a prisoner of war by the Yankees, and transferred to Johnson's Island. A person appointed by a Captain to do a particular duty, if taken, is regarded as a prisoner of war. I believe this to be the recognized rule of the service. I did not know Colcock, Collector at Charleston.

Cross-examined by Mr. Wetmore: "If I wanted a person to do a particular duty, and was deficient in officers, I should appoint some person of less rank for the time being; then he would hold the higher rank only in the discharge of that particular duty. In our volunteer service, officers and men frequently mess together. I don't know that in any exchange of prisoners, a Private is given for an Officer."

"I know, however, that the Federals hold four hundred persons at Johnson's Island, who prior to the new organization of the regiments held commissions, but afterwards, having been voted out, occupied the position of private citizens, with a view to their exchange for officers. I could make an orderly Sergeant a Captain to do a particular duty in event of there being no Lieutenant. The person appointed to discharge a particular duty in this way would be respected and obeyed by the men.

These appointments are not officially notified to the General in command, except by the regular morning's reports. If a General came along and heard of the appointment of a subaltern in the manner described, he

93

would recognize it. Never heard of Braine except in connection with the *Chesapeake* affair. Don't recollect that name among the army officers. There are so many officers in the service that it is impossible to remember the names of them all."

EVIDENCE OF E. TOM OSBORNE.

Ephraim Tom Osborne, sworn: — "I belong to Kentucky. I'm in the Confederate service. Have been serving with Gen. John H. Morgan since he was a Captain. The Yankees call him a guerilla. I have been in active service two years. I was on detached service the rest of the time. I was taken prisoner on the l9th July last, and then escaped from Camp Douglas on the 2nd Dec. last. Gen. Morgan escaped from Columbus, Ohio, previously. According to the practice of our service, officers commissioned to a particular post, or to do a particular duty, have power to delegate their authority to others; I have known it to be the case. One year ago this winter I saw it done almost every day. The reports of such appointments are made to the Colonel and from them to his superior, and so on until it goes to headquarters."

[Mr. Wetmore here observed that these reports were most likely going on yet, to which the witness observed they might stop when they reached Richmond. The quiet yet cutting way in which this retort was given caused some merriment in Court.]

"When persons so appointed have been taken prisoners they have been treated as prisoners of war. I arrived here this morning. All of our party arrived this morning. I have seen some account of the *Chesapeake* affair in the papers."

EVIDENCE OF EBEN LOCKE.

Eben Locke, sworn:—"I'm a Nova Scotian and a sea-faring man. Am a Captain and Shelburne, Nova Scotia, is my native place. Have a brother called Vernon G. Locke who goes by the name of Capt. Parker. He left Nova Scotia, about twenty years ago when a boy. He has been living in the States ever since. Believe his family live in Fayetteville, N. C. I have been in Wilmington. N. C. Was in Nassau this summer. Saw there a Confederate vessel called the *Retribution*. She was called a privateer. She had the Confederate flag flying. Saw there my brother in command of the *Retribution,* passing under the name of Capt. John Parker, He was received and recognized as Captain. He showed me his commission as I asked him to do so. I asked him either for his Commission or letters of Marque. The paper placed in my hand is the one he showed me at that time. It is in the same state now as it was then. I remember the writing on the back distinctly. My brother was on board of my vessel at Nassau. Had not seen him for 20 years. In consequence of what I heard at Nassau, I found that Capt. Parker was my brother. Next saw him at Sambro, N. S. He was then in command of the *Chesapeake* He was the same Capt. Parker, my brother, whom I saw at Nassau. I saw this same commission in his own hand in Halifax. How it got into your hands I don't know."

Cross-examined by Mr. Tuck: — "I read part of the paper. Read enough of it to know that that is the same paper. Don't know why my brother changed his name. Don't know that my brother sailed out of Boston. Know that he sailed out of New York, and out of Cape Cod. Don't know how long since he sailed out. Never saw the *Chesapeake*. I went down from Halifax to Sambro; half an hour before I arrived she had left. I never changed my name. I stayed two hours at Sambro. My brother remained till I went to Halifax. Got a carriage and brought my brother there; then went home, 60 miles east of Halifax. Don't know where my brother now is. I don't know anything about Braine or Parr and have not heard of Parker since leaving Halifax. I got none of the cargo at Sambro, nor did any of my family. I did not see any of the cargo belonging to the *Chesapeake.* My brother did not tell me of selling parts of the cargo all along the shore."

Reexamined by Mr. Gray: — "My brother is a Nova Scotian by birth. He told me his family was at Fayetteville."

Some questions put by the learned Counsel as to the conversation he had with his brother were objected to.

The Queen's Proclamation **of the 13th May, 1861**, as to the observance of neutrality pending the hostilities between the United States and the Confederate States of America, was put in evidence by Mr. Gray.

February 10th, 1864.

John Driscoll, being acquainted with Capt. Parker's handwriting, proves the signature to order to Braine, and also to commission to Collins.

W. C. Watson produced the register of the *Kate Hale,* a Confederate vessel, registered in Charleston, South Carolina, and by comparison proves the hand writing of *W.* P. Colcock, Collector of Charleston, to the endorsement on the letters of marque.

The evidence for the defense here closed.

February 15, 1864.

Mr. Gray moved for the discharge of the prisoners, on a variety of grounds; but as they appear in the argument before His Hon. Mr. Justice Ritchie, together with the authorities cited in support of them, they are omitted, except the following authorities which were not cited by the Counsel before the Judge.

After hearing Mr. Gray and Mr. Weldon, in support of these objections, and Mr. Wetmore, on the other side, the Police Magistrate adjourned to

February 24.th, 1864.

When His Worship gave the following judgment:

After recapitulating the evidence he proceeded as follows;

In giving judgment in the case, I shall first consider the effect of the evidence given on behalf of the prosecution, and what it discloses: 1st. It discloses the fact that the prisoners and a number of persons met together in Lower Cove, in the City of St. John, without authority from this or any other Government, and came to the conclusion to proceed to New York and take a steamer, the design being that they were to take passage on board of the steamer and capture her on her voyage—**the work, I say, of a coward and a villain**, which ought to be considered **as against all law—Human or Divine.** This was accomplished, and the vessel seized, as appears by the evidence.

Now upon examination of the law between a master mariner and his passenger it will be found that the grave responsibility of the person to whose skill and conduct life and property are entrusted on the ocean, and the situations of unforeseen emergency in which he may be compelled to exert himself for the passengers preservation, render it necessary that he should be invested with large, and, for the time at least, unfettered authority. Obedience to this authority, in all matters within its scope, is a duty which should be cheerfully

97

discharged by every passenger on board the ship. Whatever is necessary for the security of the vessel, the discipline of the crew, the safety of all on board, the master may require not only of the ship's company, who have expressly contracted to obey him, but of those also whom he has engaged to carry to their destination, on the implied condition of their submission to his rule. Therefore a passenger, who is found on board in time of danger, is bound, at the Master's call, to do works of necessity in defense of the ship if attacked, and for the preservation of the lives of all onboard.

Now I shall consider the effect of the evidence, and what it discloses, produced on behalf of the prisoners, touching the seizure of the *Chesapeake.*

1st: **It appeared that a most terrible civil war was existing** between the Federal States and the revolted Confederate States, and that they have been recognized by Great Britain as belligerents.

2nd. That the authority to seize and take the *Chesapeake* rests entirely on the authority and position which John Parker, *alias* Vernon G. Locke, held under the authority of the Confederate States. **Now what was his position and what authority had he from the Confederate States** to authorize him to commission persons in New Brunswick to commit this act? Does the talk at the meetings at Lower Cove about the Confederate service and officers of the Confederate service, and the presenting the Letters of Marque, give Parker, *alias* Locke, any power. I apprehend not. From the fact of Vernon G. Locke having possessed himself of the Letters of Marque at Nassau, a British port, constituting the vessel *Retribution* a private, not a public, armed vessel, in the Confederate service, whereof Thomas B. Power was commander, and there appearing on the back thereof an endorsement transferring the command of the *Retribution* to John Parker, and he, Locke, having assumed the name of John Parker, and there being no authority shown for making this transfer or that Locke was the person to whom it was in fact made, does not, I apprehend, give Locke the power on behalf of the Confederate States, to plan in the Province of New Brunswick the expedition, and create at will, officers for the Confederate service during the pendency of the war.

Now this brings me to the questions which I have to decide.

1st. There are the proceedings had before his Excellency, and his warrant in this matter. I decide that the jurisdiction given to His Excellency under the Imperial Act is not a subject matter for me to enquire into.

2d. As to my own jurisdiction. I hold that under the 10th section of the Treaty, and the Imperial Act, I have jurisdiction in cases of piracy, and that this jurisdiction extends to piracy committed on board of American vessels on the high seas, as well as for piracy committed against the municipal laws of the United States. I have carefully examined the authorities cited upon this latter point, namely: Piracy by the law of nations and piracy by the municipal law of the States. I find it stated in a note in "Wheaton" that in the construction of the British Treaty of Extradition, a crime committed at sea on board of an American vessel has been considered the same as if committed in the territory of the United States.

"Vattel" says that the domain of a nation extends to all its just possessions, and by its possession, we are not to understand its territories only, but all the rights it enjoys. He also considers **the vessels of a nation on the high seas a portion of its territories.**

The other points raised I have carefully considered, and have endeavored to search out a justification for the act perpetrated by the prisoners at the Bar and the other persons charged, and 1 must confess I can find no justification.

Taking the whole circumstances of the capture of the *Chesapeake* it was not jure *belli,* but she was seized and carried away *anima furandi.* It was not a belligerent capture but a robbery on the high seas. Therefore I consider—

1st. That this is an act of piracy;

2d. That it is justiciable by the Federal judiciary and therefore,

3d. I consider this to be rightfully a case of extradition.

It now only remains for me to declare to you **David Collins**, and to you **James McKinney**, and to you **Linus Seely**, **that I shall commit you on the charge of piracy** to the Common Jail of the City and County of Saint John, there to remain until you are **handed over to the United States authorities**, pursuant to the requisition made to His Excellency.

The Police Magistrate having issued a warrant of commitment, in accordance with his decision, the prisoners were committed to the jail of the City of Saint John, and an application being at once made to His Honor, Mr. Justice Ritchie, he issued an order in the nature of a habeas corpus under 19 Vie. Cap. 42, returnable before him at the Judge's Chambers, in the Law Society's rooms, in St. John, on the 26th February.

February 26th, 1864.

James A. Harding, Esq., High Sheriff of the City and County of Saint John, attended before Judge Ritchie, and made his return to the order of the Judge.

The order and return having been filed and read,

GRAY, Q. C, applied on the part of the prisoners, for an order to the Police Magistrate to produce the evidence and proceedings, taken before him on which the warrant for the commitment of the prisoners was issued. He referred to Act 6, W. 4, c. 36, "for more effectually securing the liberty of the subject by enforcing the execution of writs of habeas corpus;" under which the Judge before whom the return was made, was authorized to examine into the truth of the facts set forth in the return—even when that was sufficient and the Act 19, V. c 42, "for better securing the liberty of the subject" under which the order in this case had been issued, which gave the Judge enlarged powers, enacting (S. 3) that " upon return to such " order, the Judge may proceed to examine into and decide " upon the legality of the imprisonment, and make such order, "require such verification, and direct such notices or further returns in respect thereof as he may deem necessary or proper for the purposes of justice, and may, and he is hereby empowered by order in writing signed as aforesaid, to require the immediate discharge from prison, or may direct the bailment of such prisoner in such manner and for such purpose, and with the like effect and proceeding, as is now allowed upon Habeas Corpus."

RITCHIE J. — "I think some facts should be shown on affidavit to authorize my making the order asked for. I have no judicial knowledge of the proceedings before the magistrate.

GRAY, Q. C, referred to the language of the Act giving the Judge the power to order the evidence to be brought before him, even if the warrant of commitment were sufficient. The Act should have a construction in favour of liberty. There was a distinction between applications before and after indictment. Where an indictment has been found the Court cannot go behind it. But on a commitment before indictment, it is otherwise. People *v.* Martin, 1 Parker, Crim. R. 187.

RITCHIE J.—I have no doubt I may make the order, but do not think I ought to do so until some reasons are brought before me on affidavit I must presume everything to be correct.

GRAY, Q. C, stated he would obtain an affidavit if required; none could however be made before the return to the order was filed, and the only reason for making the present application was to save unnecessary delay. The Police Magistrate had received notice to produce the papers required.

On the 27th February

GRAY Q. C, applied for an order to the Police Magistrate to produce the proceedings and depositions taken in this case, on an affidavit of David Collins one of the Prisoners, stating that they were confined by virtue of a warrant issued by the Police Magistrate of Saint John, on a charge of Piracy, that the warrant was founded on certain depositions taken before the said Magistrate, by which it appeared that the offence, if any, was committed on the high seas, and without the jurisdiction of this Province and the United States, that no charge had been made on proceedings commenced against any of the prisoners, for Piracy or otherwise in any Court of the United States, that they were acting

102

under due authority from the Confederate States of America, and not Pirates, but belligerents acting against the United States *jure belli,* that no requisition by the proper authorities in the United States had been made to justify the proceeding taken against the prisoners; and also stating that the facts set out in the warrant of commitment were not supported by' the evidence adduced

He cited Archibold's Criminal Practice by Waterman, v. 1, pages 220, 2, 3, People *v* Martin, 1 Parker's Crim. R. 187. id. 1.

WETMORE Q. C, for the prosecution objected that this proceeding took place under the Imperial Statute passed to give effect to the Ashburton Treaty and not a habeas corpus act.

RITCHIE J. I am proceeding not under a habeas corpus nor the Imperial Statute referred to, but under an act giving me like powers upon an order issued under the act as in a proceeding upon habeas corpus.

I have no doubt this is a proceeding which peculiarly calls for the interposition of the highest tribunals of the land. It is the duty of Her Majesty's Justices to see that the liberty of Her subjects is preserved. If the court will interfere in the case of persons committed for trial in this Country, *a fortiori* the court will interfere where the parties are to be sent abroad. The only English case I am aware of under the extradition Statutes is one which arose under that passed to carry out the Treaty with France, (In re Besset, 6 Q. B. 481) where the court held that their powers, being statutory, were to have a strict construction. I cannot doubt I have power to .review the proceedings before the Magistrate, and if there was no ground for those proceedings, or the Magistrate has fallen into' any error, either in form or substance, and I should be of opinion the parties are illegally imprisoned, to discharge them. I think I should be failing in one of the most important of my duties did I not order not only the warrant, but also, as an affidavit has been made before me that the evidence did not warrant the conclusion the Magistrate arrived at, the depositions and proceedings before him to be brought up ; and I consider it my duty, in the words of the act to " examine into and decide upon the legality of the Imprisonment," and, the return being questioned "to require such verification" as I may deem necessary, and, to enable me so to examine and decide. I think I ought to "direct the further returns" asked for to be made.

The depositions being then handed in by Mr. Gilbert, and being read, including the charge contained in the heading of the depositions, the case was then fully argued before the learned Judge, on Saturday the 27th February, and the following Monday, Tuesday, and Wednesday.

GRAY, Q. C, and 0. *W.* WELDON, for the prisoners.

The proceedings have taken place under the Imperial Act 6 & 7, V. c. 76, (2 R. S. 429,) passed to give effect to the Ashburton Treaty. The treaty is entitled " A treaty to settle and define the boundaries etc.—and for the giving up of criminal fugitives from justice in certain cases," and the 10th Article provides for the extradition of persons charged with the commission of the crimes specified, within the jurisdiction of either country, and seeking an asylum, or being found within the territories of the other. But the treaty could give no power in itself to any officers in this Province, to act in such cases. Their powers must come from the statute and from it alone.

104

And since a man who has committed no crime in the Country where he is, is entitled to his freedom, and a man who has committed a crime against the Laws of that Country is entitled to be tried by its Courts; a statute such as this, being in derogation of these Common Law rights, must be construed strictly (In re Besset 6 Q. B. 485.) The statute provides (s. 1) that if requisition shall be made "*by the authority* of the said United States" for the delivery of any person "*charged*" with an offence committed "within *the jurisdiction*

of the United States" and found within the territories of Her Majesty ; the Lieutenant Governor shall signify that *such requisition* has been *so made,* and require "all Justices of the Peace and *other Magistrates, and officers of Justice within their several jurisdictions*" to aid in apprehending the persons so accused; and that thereupon "any Justice of the Peace or *other person* having power to commit for trial, persons accused of crimes against the Laws of that part of Her Majesty's Dominions in which such supposed offender may be found"; may examine into the charge and commit the accused person to jail until delivered up, pursuant to the requisition.

Under the provision of this statute, a warrant of commitment should show upon its face.

(1) That a requisition had been made by the authority of the United States.

(2.) That the offence was committed within the jurisdiction of the United States, and that must be their exclusive or territorial jurisdiction.

(3.) That the committing Magistrate had jurisdiction over the charge.

(4.) That the evidence taken before the Magistrate, was such as according to the laws of this Province, would justify the apprehension and committal of the persons accused if the crime had been committed in this Province, and upon such finding the warrant, should order the committal.

But the warrant of commitment in this case is defective in the following particulars.

(1.) It does not state that the evidence before the Magistrate was such as would have been sufficient to justify an apprehension and committal for trial in this Province, and thereupon under the committal.

(2.) It does not allege the offence charged was committed in the United States, or within its jurisdiction. It simply alleges that Cape Cod is in the United States.

(3.) It shows the offence to have been committed on the high seas, 20 miles off Cape Cod, and beyond the territorial jurisdiction of the United States, and directs the prisoners to be detained "until delivered up pursuant to the requisition etc." Whereas for an offence committed on the high seas, *per se* the Prisoners are justiciable in the Courts here, and **cannot be delivered up or discharged** otherwise than by due course of law here.

(4.) It shows on its face that the Magistrate who committed, was acting simply as a Justice of the Peace, and not as a commissioner or officer under the Imperial Statutes for the trial of crimes and offences committed on the high seas, and the commission for that purpose in force in this Province and **therefore it shows that the case was without his jurisdiction**, and does not come within the Imperial Act to give effect to the Treaty.

(5). It does not allege or show that any complaint or proceeding had been taken or was pending in the foreign state or that the foreign state had made any application for the rendition of the prisoners under the Treaty, or that the application was made by the *authority* of the United States.

(6). It should not only show that the offence charged was committed **within the jurisdiction of the United States**, but should go further and negative any coordinate jurisdiction which co-ordinate jurisdiction must be inferred from the **allegation of the piracy being committed on the high seas**.

And two minor objections are—

(7). There is no allegation that the evidence was taken in the presence or hearing of the prisoners.

(8). There is no allegation that the place where the evidence was taken was within the City and County of Saint John.

The warrant does not set forth the grounds of the commitment.

A mere averment that it was issued "upon due proof as by the statute required" is insufficient. Nash's case 4 B, **and** Ald. 295. And so of the averment in the present case "upon the evidence before me taken on oath." And the form of warrant given in In re Kane's 14, Howard, 77, and the terms of the Canadian Act (consol. Stats. Canada c. 89,) passed to give effect to the extradition Treaty is to the same effect.

It is perfectly consistent with the terms of the warrant in this case that there was no evidence sufficient to justify the commitment by the laws of this Province. A particular kind of evidence is required by the statute. And where a person is committed on a special authority, the commitment must be special and follow the authority. **Here there is nothing to show the nature of**

the evidence or that there was any sufficient evidence at all. Ex parte Anderson Jurist, March 16, 1861, Ed. portion p. 110.

The warrant shows no proper jurisdiction of the United States over the offence. It alleges the parties were charged with having "on the high seas 20 miles N. N. E. of Cape Cod in the United States of America, with force and arms," &c. And the jurisdiction is sought to be inferred from the *Chesapeake* being a registered United States vessel, owned by a U. S. citizen. And even then **there is nothing in the warrant to show Capt. Willet was legally in charge of the vessel.**

Nor can the exclusive jurisdiction be inferred from the *Chesapeake* being a United States vessel. The jurisdiction of every nation extends " to the punishment of piracy and other offences against the law of nations, by whomsoever and *wheresoever* committed." Lawrence's, Wheaton's, Intl. law 2d Ed. p. 231. A pirate is of no country and liable to be tried wherever he may be found, and wherever he may be arrested that country takes jurisdiction of his crime. U. S. f Palmer, 4 Curtis, 314, In re. Kane, 14 Howard, 77.

The warrant should show on its face, that the Magistrate had jurisdiction. Kite and Lane's case 1 B. and C. 101 In re Peerless 1 Q. B., 143. Ordinary Justices of the Peace have no jurisdiction over piracy. The imperial Act refers to this when it says it shall be lawful for the Lt. Governor to require " all Justices of the Peace and *other Magistrates and officers of justice within their several jurisdictions"* to aid in apprehending persons charged, and further that it shall be lawful "for any Justice of the Peace or *other persons* having power to commit for trial," to examine into the truth of the charge alleged. The only authority in this Province to try charges of piracy is under the Imperial Statutes 28 Hen. 8 c 15 and 11 and 12 *W*. 3 c
108

7 and under those statutes a commission has been issued and is in force. And the commission only extends to the persons named in it and not to all Magistrates within the Province. Special Statutes have given justices power to act in England 7 Bac Abr p. 446. Title Piracy 7, Qeo. 4 c 38; but there is no such authority to Justices here.

Justices of the Peace as such have no jurisdiction on the high seas. By the terms of their appointment in this Province their jurisdiction is confined to the County for which they are appointed. The Governor's warrant could give no jurisdiction.

The Canadian statute specially authorizes Justices of the Peace to act in such cases, but the Imperial Statutes does not, but limits the action of the respective officers "within their several jurisdictions."

The Lieutenant Governor is bound to pursue the terms of the act and until a proper requisition is made he cannot issue a legal warrant. But the requisitions of the United States Consul in the present case as shown in the recital in the warrant of commitment are not sufficient. They do not even assert the application to be made "by the authority" but only "on behalf" of the United States terms entirely different since an application may be made on behalf of another without his knowledge, and such an application would fix him with no liability. It may be adopted or repudiated as the party principal chooses. Nor does it appear that the right to make such requisitions is vested in the American Consul *virtute officio*—-nor is any direct authority or instructions to him, or any subsequent ratification of his actions shown—nor if shown, could it cure the defect.

The warrant states the parties were brought up "to answer the complaint of Isaac Willett of the State of New York," and not a complaint made by authority of the United States.

That complaint of Willett's was made in this Province, and not in the United States It was made before a magistrate who had no jurisdiction in cases of piracy. If he had power to take such a complaint where was the use of the Lieut. Governor's warrant at all. The whole proceedings were *coram non judice.*

The requisition should be made by the executive authority.

Opinions of the U. S. Attorney General cited in Wheaton's Int. Law, pp. 241, 2.—Notes—In re Kane, 14, Howard, 77, and the terms of the Canadian Statutes are to the same effect.

The U. S. Consul's requisitions refer to no such authority. It is consistent with their terms that he merely applied to have the parties tried here. Nor does it appear that the parties had been legally" charged" in the United States as required by the terms of the statute. The requisitions merely say the parties were "believed to be guilty." The second section of the Imperial Act refers to "the depositions upon-which the original warrant was granted," showing that their existence is necessary. And in re Kane, 14, Howard, 77, and Metzger's case, 1 Parker, C. 188, are to the same effect. Here even if the prisoners were taken to the boundary line, for all that appears on the warrant of commitment, there would be no one authorized on the part of the United States to receive them—no warrant issued there on which they could be detained.

This proceeding though on its face a mere commitment for trial **is a quasi-conviction**, since the Magistrate commits the parties to be handed over to another jurisdiction and **deprived of rights they would here enjoy,** and the warrant should therefore be construed with the **utmost strictness**.

But leaving the questions as to the validity of the warrant, and taking up the facts which appeared in evidence, the prisoners are entitled to their discharge on the following grounds:—

First. The offence charged is Piracy on the High Seas. It is therefore cognizable by the proper tribunals of the Country, and the parties committed do not come within the Extradition Treaty with the United States:—

(1). The jurisdiction which a nation has over its public and private vessels on the high seas, is exclusive only so far as respects offences against its own municipal laws. **Piracy and murder on the high seas are punishable by the Law of Nations wherever the criminal may be found**, and no Country has exclusive jurisdiction of such offences.

(2). No Country can make that Piracy which is not Piracy by the Law of Nations, in order to give jurisdiction to its own courts over such offences.

(3). The Extradition Treaty between the United States and Great Britain, contemplates only a demand and delivery in cases where the crime committed **falls exclusively** within the jurisdiction of the Country demanding, and is not applicable where a co-ordinate jurisdiction to try and punish for the crime committed exists in the Country where the person demanded is found. Therefore, if the taking of the *Chesapeake* be Piracy under the Law of Nations, the tribunals of this Country can take cognizance of the crime, and the party charged can neither be demanded nor legally given up.

111

Second. Under the relative positions which the United States and the Confederate States bear to each, other—both having been recognized as belligerents by Her Majesty's Government—the offence is not Piracy at all; the parties committed are in no way punishable, and cannot be surrendered:—

(1). It is not Piracy, because open war exists between the revolted Country of the Confederate States and the United States, and in such case the Law of Nations does not regard acts of aggression done by the Subjects of the revolted Country against the persons, property or commerce of the parent Country as piracy or murder, and the same immunity is extended to all who aid or are acting with them *bona fide* in the act committed.

(2), The circumstances of the case show conclusively that the parties seizing and taking the *Chesapeake*, in so doing, **were not acting as Pirates** *eum animo depredandi caul furandi,* **but as belligerents** seeking to **capture and destroy the property of an enemy**, and acting in the name of, and on behalf of the revolted Country.

(8). It is not even necessary in such cases that the party acting should be commissioned by his Government—that is simply a matter between himself and his own Government, and affects him so far only as it vests the property captured in the Government and not in the captor. **It is only necessary to prove two facts—** first, the **existence of open war; second, that the act done was "not for piratical purposes, but in the furtherance of a belligerent object.**

(4). Great Britain having recognized the Confederate States as belligerents, the Subjects of the Confederate States must be regarded *quoad hoe* as ceasing to be Subjects of the United States, and not

112

bound by its municipal laws; so that even though the seizure and taking of the *Chesapeake* might, in a Subject of the United States be piracy, yet.it cannot be so in a Subject of the Confederate States or those acting with them.

(5). The term Piracy used in the Treaty must be regarded as used in a sense which would not clash with the Law of Nations; not as used in the sense created for it by the municipal law of a particular Country. **Thus the Law of Nations does not regard acts committed by belligerents as piratical**; though the Country against which the acts have been com mitted may have passed a law that those acts are piratical.

The word "piracy" as used in the Treaty must have reference to acts for which there is no punishment in the Country to which the party charged has escaped, but which in that Country, if committed there, would nevertheless be considered as piracy; for instance certain offences in harbors etc. In the present case, the offence being on the High Seas, cannot come within the latter class, and **Great Britain having recognized the Confederate States as belligerents**, they cannot come within the former.

(6.) Officers and men having no permanent connection with the Country, or interest in its cause, are and may be privateers, and **cannot be treated us pirates**, and fraud may be employed as well as force.

(7.) The Courts of a neutral Government which recognizes the existence of a civil war in another Country, **cannot consider as criminal those acts of hostility which war authorizes**, and which the new Government may direct against its enemies.

113

Third. The Court of a Justice of the Peace has no jurisdiction in cases like the present, and a Justice of the Peace as such, has no power either to investigate or commit:

(1.) A Justice of the Peace has no jurisdiction or authority to issue a warrant or hold an investigation, and the Governor can give no such authority.

(2.) The warrant issued in this Province, must be based upon preliminary proceedings, had before a competent tribunal in the United States, having jurisdiction of the offence, and **showing that the criminal acts charged were committed within the territorial jurisdiction of the United States**, which proceedings must be forwarded to the Governor of this Province, before the Governor can issue his warrant, in order to give any tribunal or authority in this Province, jurisdiction to enquire into the offence.

(3.) On the face of the warrant to apprehend the prisoners, **it discloses no requisition made by the proper authorities** of the United States, by its authority, as required by the treaty, and is therefore invalid.

(4.) **It does not show that in the United States any complaint has been lodged**, or proceeding taken against the parties charged, on which the proceedings in this Province cm be based, and is therefore on that account invalid.

(5.) The warrant to apprehend the **prisoners is defective in combining two crimes** which are triable before separate and distinct tribunals.

(6,) The authority to a Magistrate to act, is limited to such crimes as could be committed in that part of the kingdom in which the Magistrate resided; and as the high seas are not a part of Her Majesty's Dominions, a Justice of the Peace, in the absence of an}' specific legislation thereupon, has no jurisdiction or power to act in any matter relating to piracy; the examination and warrant in such cases must *be* before one of the officers composing the mixed Court for the trial of piracy and offences on the high seas, constituted by the Imperial Act.

Fourth. Tins expedition, starting in a neutral territory, however gross a violation of that neutrality, does not affect the status of parties engaged in that expedition, *quoad* the other belligerents, but only is illegal as regards the neutral Country whose laws have been violated.

Fifth. The evidence showing that these prisoners were enlisted in the cause of the Confederate service, under a genuine commission of that State, this neutral Court cannot enquire into the validity of that enlistment, except for offences against its own laws.

It has been urged that the *Chesapeake* being a United States ship, her deck should for all purposes be considered a portion of the United States territory.

The Police Magistrate in part based his decision upon this. But the authorities cited (Wheaton's Int. Law, p. 208, Vattel, Laws of Nations, Book 1, c 19, Sec. 216, and Book 2, c 7, Sec. 8,) do not bear out the conclusion. The jurisdiction of a nation in such case is exclusive only so far as respects offences against its own municipal laws, (Wheaton's Int. Law pp. 735, 208, 9, 256, Dictum of Cockburn, C. J., Regina *v* Heane, Times of Feb. 1st, 1864.)

The offence charged in the present case is Piracy on the high seas, there is no allegation in the warrants of any violation of the municipal laws of the United States. But Piracy by the Law of Nations was never contemplated by the Extradition Treaty or statute. It only contemplates piracy by municipal law, (Wheaton's Int. Law, p. 240, n 1.)

It could never have been intended to deprive either of the contracting parties of a jurisdiction it already possessed ; **the reason of the treaty and statute is plainly that escaping prisoners not punishable by the laws of one Country, should be delivered up to the other,** and if this crime can be punished here, that reason is at an end. If the word piracy in the statute is to have a general meaning, France might claim the jurisdiction as well as the United States. There is no necessity for the treaty as regards Piracy on the high seas. A party committing such an offence is to be tried within the jurisdiction where he is found.

And the United States Statutes as put in evidence, require that pirates should he tried in the first district in which they are taken or found, and *give* jurisdiction to that district Court alone, (8 U. S. Statutes at large, p. 514.) And no legislation jurisdiction on their part could make an offense on the high seas piracy, so as to give the Courts exclusive jurisdiction (U. S. v. Palmer, 4 Curtis 314. The Antelope, 10 Wheaton 844.}

Their Jurisdiction not being exclusive, in giving up parties triable here, we should only fool ourselves. The right to try the offence attaches in the United States only on the parties being found there; the Statute only contemplates the rendition of fugitives escaping from justice in another country which these are not.

The acts of the captors of the Chesapeake subsequent to the vessels capture cannot render their act piracy. Belligerents have no rights; their vessels and goods when captured by an enemy may be dispersed of as he pleases. Wheaton's Int. Law, pp. 629, 659, 652, 13 Howard 515.

The treaty did not contemplate civil war in the present case, the parties claimed to capture vessels for the Confederate States.

They had the color of a Commission. If a bona-fide commission it was sufficient to protect them. A belligerent may enlist men in a neutral country; though amenable to its municipal laws for doing so. The offence is only cognizable by the neutral state. An officer may be shown by his acts as well as by his Commission.

Here Parker was recognized in the British harbor of Nassau as having a letter of marque.

A person having a letter of marque implies his having men and he has a right to send his officers and men out to act on separate expeditions.

The evidence shows a bona fide enlistment in the Confederate service. A person may obtain the rights of a citizen of a foreign country without naturalization. Marryat v Wilson, 1 B. & P. 444. The *Santisima Trinidad*, 7 Wheaton, 283.

In this case Captain Parker had been for 20 years a resident in the Southern States.

Any private citizen of a belligerent has the right to destroy the enemy's property wherever found. .A commission from the belligerent government is unnecessary. Kents Coms, v 1. pp. 106, 7, 8, Wheaton's Int. Law.-p p. 252, G27. The only effect of the want of a commission is that a prize goes to the government and not to the captor. As between belligerents, any man fighting on one side is the enemy of the other. But the genuineness of the commission in the present case is undoubted. The right of Captain Parker to hold it is alone questioned. But a commission does not follow the ship. It goes to the Commander.

There is no evidence of any legal proceedings before any United Status tribunal.

No warrant appears to have been issued in the demanding country as was the case in ex parte Besset, 6 Q. B. 481, and In re Kane Curtis 64. Nor can the application be made by the Consul *virtue office*. In the United States the necessity for the prior action of the Executive is done away with by their Statute, but here it is otherwise.

And the Consul's application was only supported by a deposition not clearly charging piracy and sworn before a magistrate who in a case of piracy had no authority to take depositions at all. The proceedings must be construed *strietiesimi juris* and the warrant etc., cannot be corrected by the depositions. Ex parte Besset 6 Q.B. 481. Christie v: Unwin,11 Ad. and E.373.

An expedition organized in a neutral country is only illegal as so far as the neutral country is concerned.

The legitimacy of the use of mercenary troops has always been recognized. A familiar instance is that of Sir Delacy Evans, and the Spanish contingent. The only party to complain is the neutral whose territory or subjects are employed.

The evidence shows clearly an enlistment. However gross an infraction of neutrality, that enlistment is only punishable by our own laws.

The United States cannot complain. Had Parker been at Nassau without authority he would have been taken and punished. His commission was duly transferred from Power the *Retribution's* first Captain. The witness Calcock's signature being official must be presumed correct, the commission was shown by Parker as his authority, and the men enlisted under him in the

118

service of the Confederate States, for the purpose of waging war against the United States.'

RITCHIE J. .Assuming as you must do at this stage of your argument, the correctness of the proceedings against the prisoners, and the magistrate's jurisdiction of the offence; do not these questions fall within the province of the Superior Court on the trial of the prisoner. Is it not the Magistrate's duty now merely to see if a preliminary case is made out? I think we must act in this case just as if it was an offence committed here.

The question is would I on the evidence commit for trial in this Country.

If so, must I not commit the parties for extradition?

In Anderson's case a *prima facie* case was made out, but the prisoner was discharged. And so in U. S. *v.* Palmer, 4 Curtis, 314. Parker is found in command of the Retribution and Braine and Parr acting under him.

RITCHIE J. I think these questions are proper for a jury and not for the magistrate. His duty is simply to deal with this case as a magistrate would deal with an offence to be tried in this Country.]

The parties were only making war on the United States.

They took the vessel on the part of the Confederate States. The organization was under the color of a Confederate commission and that was sufficient.

But if all other points fail, the heading placed by the Police Magistrate to the depositions is sufficient to discharge the prisoners.

He says the prisoners were charged with having committed piracy "within the jurisdiction of the United States and the Circuit Courts thereof, and against the

119

laws of the United States, and the Statutes of the United Kingdom of Great Britain and Ireland." But by the United States Statutes put in evidence, it is clear that those Courts have no jurisdiction until the prisoner is found within their districts, and there is no evidence in this case of any such jurisdiction attaching at all. The United States by their Acts of Congress recognize that the high seas are not within that jurisdiction. Besides, the evidence varies from the Lieutenant Governor's warrant, which gives no authority to enquire into offences committed within the jurisdiction of the Circuit Courts of the United States, and against the Statutes of the United Kingdom of Great Britain and Ireland. The allegations put in by the Magistrate, were not read to the prisoners—were not charged at first. They arose out of the evidence and on the argument before the Magistrate. There is nothing in the original warrant and proceedings to support the investigation of such a charge; and unless the evidence was taken under those warrants and proceedings, it was not rightly taken at all.

WETMORE, Q. C, (with him was TUCK) for the prosecution.

Admitting the first deposition of Willett's before the Police Magistrate to have been taken without jurisdiction and *coram nonjudice,* the United States Consul's letter containing the statement of the offence, and names of the parties, and professing to be made by authority of the executive department of the United States government, is in itself sufficient. The only person to judge of the validity of the requisition is the Lieutenant Governor. If a requisition is presented to him he must decide, and no inconvenience can arise from this, as the parties are not committed to-be given up under the Governor's warrant alone. It merely authorizes an investigation.

120

The Statute does not require the requisition to be in writing. A verbal one would be sufficient. The Governor's warrant recites the treaty, and although it states that requisition had been made *on behalf of the* United States; it says also that it was made "in pursuance of the treaty" the words "on behalf of" were unnecessary. They are mere surplus words. The warrant would be sufficient if they were left out.

With regard to the Magistrate's jurisdiction in cases of piracy, the words of the Imperial Statutes are cumulative. Where it says, "It shall be lawful for any Justice of the Peace or other Person having power to commit for trial" to examine into the charge, etc., it is intended that *any* of these persons may act in the investigation of and of the offences referred to.

The Magistrate under the statute, is to examine into the charge, and this whatever it is—and wherever he may do it, it will be equally valid. It is not necessary that it should be in presence of the party. The statute authorizes the examination into the offence, even before the warrant for the apprehension of the criminal is issued.

Under the construction of the Act, the Magistrate must first issue his warrant to apprehend, and then by warrant commit the offender. No evidence subsequent to the issuing of the warrant is required. The Magistrate could, had he seen fit, have committed them on Willett's depositions alone.

The second section of the statute which enacts that "copies of the depositions upon which the original warrant was granted, certified under the hand of the person or persons issuing such warrant, and attested upon oath, may be received in evidence" does not render a preliminary proceeding in the demanding country necessary in all cases. The words are merely permissive. They legalize the use of such depositions if taken in the demanding country—do not render it necessary to take them.

The parties were duly "charged" within the terms of the statute by the United States Consul's requisition. The word "charged" in the statute does not mean any specific charge or particular form of charge. Suppose the case of proceedings before a Justice on an accusation of murder; but it appeared on investigation that the crime had been committed beyond his jurisdiction, and in the United States. There the party would be "charged" by the depositions before the Justice. And in this view the parties were "charged" by Willett's first deposition. In the form of warrant given in Besset's Case, (6 Q, B. 481) the word used is not "charged" but "accused."

The Statute does not confine the rendition *to fugitives* from the jurisdiction of the demanding Country. The words of the Treaty recited in the Statute expressly extend to all criminals who "should be found" as well as those who "should seek an asylum" within the territories of the other nation.

As to this crime having been committed on the high seas and our Courts having jurisdiction over it, there can be no doubt that the Courts of the United States have a co-ordinate jurisdiction. Having made a requisition, then they are entitled to have the criminal given up. The United States vessel was United States Territory, and the United States had full jurisdiction over her. Kent's Com. Ed. 1832, pp. 184, 6, 7. Wheaton Inter. Law pp. *203, 9,* Regina v. Heane, Times Feb. 1, '64 "The Flowery Land" London Morning Post, Feb. 5, '64.

The *Chesapeake* had a United States Register and carried the United States flag.

There is nothing in the Statute to limit the word "piracy" to municipal piracy.

If it does not mean piracy by international law it means nothing at all, and if it intends only what would be piracy by the municipal law of the United States and not here, for such an offence the parties could not be given up at all. There must be a similarity in the laws of the two Countries as to the offence.

The question of the parties holding a valid commission from the Confederate States would clearly be a matter for consideration at their final trial, and not at this preliminary stage of the proceedings; it is a question for a jury. There was no real proof of Colcock's signature to the transfer from Power to Parker.

No greater particularity can be required in the warrant in the present case, than in any proceeding in our own Courts. This is a preliminary proceeding, and no such great particularity is therefore required. Besides the proceedings may be amended.

The English decisions cited on this point by the prisoners' Counsel, do not apply. The Act under which the order was granted in this case, differs from the habeas corpus statutes, and enables the Judge to "make such order as he may deem necessary." The Magistrate's heading of the evidence is immaterial. It cannot create any variance between the Lieutenant Governor's warrant and the proceedings taken under it, or invalidate the proceedings if otherwise correct.

Gray, *Q.C. in reply*. The alteration in the heading of the evidence is very important. It saps the very foundations of justice. If a requisition is made and a warrant issued and the magistrate takes evidence on a different charge it is a serious matter. The alteration has a suspicious appearance and was made to cover an objection raised at the trial. It has a material bearing on the case. If the evidence does not correspond with the Lieut. Governor's warrant what evidence is there to show the parties are guilty at all?

In that case the parties are in jail under a commitment not supported by the evidence. If there is no evidence the commitment is irregular and illegal. If there is evidence it does not support the charge. And the proceedings cannot be amended by the evidence.

The Consul's Mere Letter Not Sufficient

As to the sufficiency of the requisition, the effect of the argument of the Counsel for the prosecution would be that a warrant for the arrest of any person, claimed to have committed an offense in the United States could be issued without any sworn depositions at all. And the evidence negates the inference drawn from the warrant's reciting it was issued in pursuance of the treaty." Surely any person calling himself an United States Consul cannot by merely writing a letter to the Lieut. Governor have a warrant issued calling on sill Magistrates to arrest any member of her Majesty's subjects the Consul may choose to name.

And under the Imperial Statute, the Lieut. Governor's warrant could not authorize the magistrate to take Willett's second deposition.

It could only authorize magistrates to act within their several jurisdictions. The United States can only be entitled to jurisdiction over piracy on the high seas when the pirates are found within their jurisdiction. If found here we have jurisdiction, and our Courts must use it.

Nothing Shows United States Jurisdiction

There is nothing to show that this particular case is, in the opinion of the United States Government or Courts, within their jurisdiction.

Had proceedings first been taken there it would have been otherwise. There is now no United States officer authorized to receive the prisoners on their being taken to the boundary. The original warrant is bad as combining two distinct offences – murder and piracy

The Learned Judge, having taken time to consider, on the 10th March, 1864, delivered the following

JUDGEMENT
IN RE:
DAVID COLLINS.
JAMES McKinney and
LINUS SEELY

This was an application made to me on behalf of the above named prisoners under the Act of Assembly for bettor securing the liberty of the subject and for sufficient cause having been shown to me, I did by order in writing the Keeper of the City and County of Saint John to return to me the said parties who were confined by the said Jail under a warrant from Humphrey T. Gilbert, Police Magistrate

McKinney from the 27th of December; Collins from the of for examination by the said Magistrate, up to 11 o'clock or thereabouts of the morning of the 24th February, then instant, when they were taken to the Office of the said Magistrate ; that the said Collins, McKinney and Seely were committed to the said Jail at mid-day on the 25th day of February, then instant, with a warrant or commitment, which the said Sheriff sets out *verbatim,* and this he returns is the cause of the detaining of the said parties whose bodies he says he has ready.

The warrant or commitment set forth is under the hand and sea! of Humphrey T. Gilbert, Esquire, a Justice of the Peace of the City and County of Saint John, and Police Magistrate for the City of Saint John, and dated 25th February, 1864.

(Vide Appendix F.)

On this return being made to me at the time appointed for the hearing of this matter, on application made on behalf of the said prisoners on the affidavit of David Collins, I did, in pursuance of the power and authority in me vested by the Act of Assembly, 19th Vic, chap. 42, require and direct a return to be made to me of all the proceedings, examinations, orders and depositions taken before H. T. Gilbert, P. M. and J. P., &c., under and by virtue of a Warrant purporting to be issued by His Excellency the Lieutenant Governor, dated the 24th Dec. 1863, the same being deemed by me necessary and proper for the purposes of Justice to enable me to examine into and decide upon the legality of the imprisonment of the said parties ; and I directed that notice of such order should be forthwith served on Mr. Gilbert, who, upon notice thereof, returned to me all such proceedings and documents before him, that is to say the Warrant from his Excellency the Lieutenant Governor, the complaint of Isaac Willett, Mr. Gilbert s first Warrant to apprehend the prisoners, the evidence and all proceedings on the part of the prosecution, and the evidence and all proceedings on the part of the prisoners, including copies of the original letters and the requisition of J. Q. Howard, Esq., U. S. Consul at the City of St. John, upon which the Warrant of His Excellency was issued, and of the original depositions of Isaac Willett and Daniel Henderson transmitted by the said

126

Consul with one of the said letters, duly certified
agreeably to the Act of Assembly, under the hand of the
Hon. S. L. Tilley, Provincial Secretary, and the charge at
length on which the examination before Mr. Gilbert
proceeded.

(Vide American Consul's letters—Appendix A.)

The depositions transmitted with one of these
letters professed to have been sworn before "H. T.
Gilbert, Police Magistrate of the City of Saint John," on
the 22nd Dec, 1863, the *Jurat* does not say where.

The depositions are headed "Province of New
Brunswick, City and County of Saint John, to wit, "and
commence" Isaac Willett of the City of New York in the
State of New York, United States of America, Captain of
the steamer " *Chesapeake*" belonging to the United
States of America, and Daniel Henderson of the City of
Portland in the State of Maine, one of the United States,
Second Mate of the said steamer," and then detail, so far
us within their own knowledge or what they heard on
board, the circumstances of the capture by certain
passengers (fifteen in all,) of whom the names of Braine,
Collins, Robinson and Parr are given, the names of the
others being unknown to them; of the steamer
Chesapeake when she was about 20 miles North North
East of Cape Cod, the shooting of the Engineer, wounding
of the Mate and Second Engineer; and the forcible taking
possession of the vessel, and the sending on shore in
New Brunswick of the Captain and all the crew except
the first and third Engineers and three Firemen, who
were retained on board; and the deponents state that
the}; are informed and fully believe that J. C. Braine, H. C.
Brooks, David Collins, John Parker Locke, *alias* John

127

Parker. Linus Seely, George Robinson, Galbraith Cox, Robert Cox, James McKinney, Robert Clifford, and H. A. Parr were among others the captors of the said steamer *Chesapeake,* a steamer of the said United States of America, on her passage from New York to Portland, and that these persons being passengers on board took forcible possession of the said steamer against their will and that of the other officers and crew of the said steamer.

But except for detailing the facts above which were referred to; no charge of Piracy or Murder is made, and no allegation whatever of the acts having been committed within the jurisdiction of the United States.

Vide .Appendix:

I for charge, touching which the witnesses were examined by Mr. Gilbert. A variety of objections were urged at length to the proceedings in this case. They are all, I think, covered by the following:

First, that there was no legal charge against the prisoners in the United States or in this Province of an offence mentioned in the Statute committed within the jurisdiction of the United States, nor any proper requisition by the authority of the United States for the rendition of the prisoners, and therefore the Governor had no authority under the treaty and statute to issue his warrant.

Secondly—That if he had, Mr. Gilbert had not, either as Police Magistrate for the City of Saint John, or as a Justice of the Peace for the City and County of Saint John, any authority to examine touching the truth of the charge of Piracy alleged in the warrant, or to commit the persons accused thereof.

Thirdly—That if Mr. Gilbert had jurisdiction, the evidence before him showed that the offence was not

128

piracy, and the prisoners were not guilty of that crime, and consequently there was no evidence of the truth of the charge, but to the contrary.

Fourthly—That if he was not wrong in this he wrongfully took a fresh complaint, and wrongfully examined on charges contained in that complaint, and not on the charge in the Governor's Warrant, and that the Warrant he issued and under which the prisoners are now detained is bad on its face and not sufficient in law to justify their detention.

The Queen has a right to know why any of Her subjects, or persons in Her dominions, who are alleged to be wrongfully imprisoned are so restrained of their liberty.

The Writ of Habeas Corpus at Common Law and by statute, and the statute of the General Assembly under which I am now acting, are the constitutional means in this Province by which all alleged improper imprisonments are enquired into, and Her Majesty's Supreme Court and the Judges of that Court are bound on proper cause shown to investigate all cases of alleged unlawful arrest, and to relieve therefrom, if shown to be contrary to law.

The right to grant such relief in this case has not been, and cannot be questioned. Having then all the proceedings before me I have to ascertain and determine whether or not such proceedings are justified by and in conformity with the Treaty and Act of Parliament. If they are, this application must be dismissed. If they are not, the prisoners must be discharged.

The Treaty, under which the delivery up to the United States Government of the prisoners is sought, is a

Treaty ratified on the l3th of October, 1843—"to settle and define the boundaries between the possessions of Her Britannic Majesty in North America and the Territories of the United States"—for the "final suppression of the African slave trade, and for giving up criminals, fugitives from Justice, in certain cases". The recital of it having reference to that portion which bears on the present case is:—"Whereas it is found expedient for the better administration of Justice and the prevention of crime within the Territories and Jurisdiction of the two parties respectively that persons committing the crimes as hereinafter enumerated, and being fugitives from Justice, should, under certain circumstances, be reciprocally delivered up". .4nd Article- X. contains the stipulation agreed on.
     (**Vide Appendix B.**)
     To enable this Treaty to be carried out in the British Dominions a statutory enactment was necessary, and the Parliament of Great Britain in the 6th and 7th year of Her Majesty's reign passed an Act for giving effect to the Treaty, which after reciting the 10th article of the Treaty, and the 11th with reference to the duration of this portion of it, after reciting that it is expedient that provision should be made for carrying the said agreement into effect, enacts as follows:
     —**Vide Appendix C.**
     The authority which this statute gives the other administering the Government of any Colony and all Justices of the Peace and other Magistrates and
     Officers of Justice within their several jurisdictions to act being a statutory power, they must one and all act strictly in accordance with the authority given, and rigidly pursue that authority. Bearing this in mind, I proceed to the consideration of the first objection. We must look closely to the Act of Parliament, for it is from that, and
130

that alone, the authority to act proceeds, and the very first words of the enacting part of the statute show that the basis of this right is on an event.

In case Requisition shall at any time be made by the authority of the United States in pursuance of and according to the said Treaty for the delivery of any person charged with (certain crimes including Piracy) committed within the jurisdiction of the United States. Thus we see the Requisition is not to be a simple bold request for the delivery up of the person named, but it is a Requisition which must be by the authority of the U. S.—it must be in pursuance of and in accordance with the Treaty—it must be for the delivery of a person charged with one of the offences mentioned in the Treaty, and the offence with which he is charged must have been committed within the jurisdiction of the United States.

If a case perfect in all these ingredients is presented, the statute says it shall be lawful for the Administrator of the Government of any Colony or Possession by a Warrant under his hand and seal, to signify that such requisition has been made. Deficient in any one of these statuary requirements the Governor is powerless to act.

Let us therefore examine the documents upon which His Excellency issued his Warrant in this case. They all bear date on the same day, and in the absence of any evidence to the contrary, I may assume were laid before His Excellency at the same time, but the letter signed .1. Q. Howard, *V.* S. Consul, in which the prisoners are named, would appear to have been the first written. It is a communication addressed to the Lieut. Governor through the Provincial Secretary. The first part of this letter is simply a request that the Governor will use his authority under the Act of Parliament "to the end that certain offenders (not naming them or their crime, or the place or jurisdiction within which committed) may be apprehended and delivered up to Justice" (not stating to whom.)

It then proceeds to desire the Secretary to make known to His Excellency that as an officer of the United States Government the writer is authorized by the Executive Department of that Government to make a Requisition upon him as the officer administering the Government of this Province, in order that certain persons (not naming them) believed (not charged) to be guilty of the crime of Piracy (not stating within what jurisdiction committed, and not stating whether piracy against the law of nations or piracy against the municipal laws of any particular country) may be brought before the proper officers of .justice, so that the evidence of their guilt or innocence may be heard and considered; and then he requests that, in accordance with the provisions of the said Act of Parliament, His Excellency will by Warrant signify that a Requisition has been made for the apprehension of John C Braine and others, including the prisoners, and require that all Justices of the Peace and other Magistrates within the jurisdiction of this Province shall aid in apprehending the above named persons accused (not charged) of the crime of piracy, for the purpose not of having them delivered up, but for the purpose of having them brought to trial. Under the statute we have seen the Requisition must be made "by the authority of the United States", that is of the Government of the United States.

Had Mr. Howard been a public Minister of the United States, and so the representative of that

Government, a Requisition by him would doubtless have been good; but I am not aware that as Consul he had any such authority unless specially delegated. Perhaps the fair construction of that letter would be that Mr. Howard intended to convey to the Governor that he was so specially authorized, but the authority he claims is simply " in order that certain persons believed to be guilty of the crime of piracy may be brought before the proper officers of Justice, so that the evidence of their guilt or innocence may be heard and considered."

This is all that he puts forward as to the extent of his authority, and upon this, without production of the authority, he proceeds to request that His Excellency will by Warrant signify as before stated. No authority from the Government of the United States is shown or directly alleged authorizing him to ask for the apprehension of the individual parties he names, or to ask for their apprehension as charged with the crime committed within the jurisdiction of the United States, but simply of parties accused of the crime of piracy, for the purpose not of being delivered up under the Treaty, but for the purpose of having them brought to trial. Had His Excellency issued such a Warrant as is here asked for, I have no hesitation in saying, for the reasons that will hereafter be given in considering another branch of this case, it would have been bad. Is the matter then helped by the second letter? By this letter the Consul transmits affidavits of the Captain and second Mate, sworn at St. John before H. T. Gilbert, Police Magistrate, on no charge or complaint, to be presented to His Excellency in case "he requires evidence of the criminality of the persons charged with the crime of Piracy before issuing the

133

Warrant for having them brought to trial". A sincere hope is then expressed that no obstacle will be thrown in the way of bringing those charged with so grave an offence to justice. If there are deficiencies in the first, it can hardly be urged that they are supplied by this letter or by the depositions accompanying it.

His Excellency being one of the Commissioners named in the Royal Commission for taking information and apprehending and committing for trial persons charged with offences on the high seas, and if brought to trial, one of the Judges to try them, this letter instead of being a Requisition under the statute, or in aid of a Requisition, if I may use the expression, more resembles an application to His Excellency in that capacity than to him under the 6th and 7th Vic., as an officer administering the Government, more particularly as the last paragraph, says : "We had believed until this late hour that a Requisition before the Executive would not have been required in the first instance," which would rather corroborate the view that proceedings were desired, independent of a requisition.

As to the depositions in my opinion it cannot make the requisition good if not good without it.

It appears to have been sworn before Mr. Gilbert as Police Magistrate, and was, I think on his part wholly extra judicial. No complaint or information appears to have been laid before him to justify his taking the deposition, and if the charge of Piracy, which the statements in it unanswered would justify, had been made at that time before him, he had no jurisdiction to entertain it; still less had he jurisdiction if the offence was an alleged crime committed within the jurisdiction of the United States, and therefore amounted to no legal charge, and to no legal evidence of the crime of Piracy ; but is it not absolutely necessary that the parties should be charged with the commission within the jurisdiction of the United States of one of the crimes mentioned, that is legally charged judicially, or by public process, or in some manner warranted by the laws of the country in which the alleged offence was committed. I think the words of the statute too clear to admit of any reasonable doubt on this point; and the 2nd section of the Act confirms me in this view. This Section contemplates it being done by the issuing of a warrant, for in providing that certain evidence may be used by the Magistrate or officer in the investigation of the criminality of the person apprehended, it says, "copies of the depositions upon which the original warrant was granted."

This obviously refers to the original warrant granted in the country where the crime was committed and anterior to the requisition; and this view would seem to be entertained by jurists of the highest celebrity in the United States, for in the judgment of Nelson, Justice, in the Supreme Court of the United States in Kane's case, as reported in 14 Howard, he says; "This species of evidence is very differently guarded in the Act of Parliament, 6th and 7th Vic. There, copies of the depositions laid before the Government, and upon which the proper officer issued his warrant to the Magistrates authorizing them to institute proceedings to arrest and commit the fugitive, are those only permitted to be given in evidence; in other words, copies of the depositions upon which the Government acted in the matter are admissible as evidence of criminality. The original of these are those upon which our Government makes the requisition, and of course the good faith of the nation is pledged that they are taken before competent officers, and that the

135

facts stated are true." And Chief Justice Taney concurring, as he said he did, in all that Nelson, Justice, then said, contented himself with expressing his entire assent to the opinion Nelson had then just delivered; and Daniel, Justice, concurred in all that Nelson, Justice said. And that this principle has been acted on will be seen by reference to Besset's case, 6 Ad., and El., in England, where we find a warrant was first issued in France, and to Kane's in the United States, just referred to, where a warrant was issued in Ireland, in addition to the special authority and affidavit of the Consul. In Kane's case, reported in 14 Howard, Mr. Barclay, the British Consul was specially employed, the report says, by direct authority of the British Minister, accredited to the Government of the United States, and in pursuance of this authority Mr.

Barclay made the necessary affidavit; and no case has been cited to me, nor am I aware of any, where a different practice has been adopted. On the contrary I find in a note to the last edition by Lawrence of Wheaton's International Law, this view confirmed by the opinion of Mr. Gushing, May 21st, 1854, in the published opinions of the Attorneys General of the United States, volume 6, page 485, **The practice is declared by him in these words** :—

"The practice of our own Government, as well as that of Great Britain, requires that all claims of Extradition should be founded on a judicial warrant, with proper evidence to justify the warrant. The United States will not, therefore, make a demand on Great Britain for a person alleged to be a fugitive from the justice of one of the United States without the exhibition of a judicial warrant issued on sufficient proof by the local authority." And again, in an opinion by the same learned gentleman, Nov. 2, 1854, published in the same work, vol. 7, page 6,

136

he says: "A mere notification from a foreign legation that a party guilty of a crime has escaped, and perhaps fled to the United States of America, is not sufficient to justify the preliminary action of the President. The general rule is, the Government of which extradition, whether by comity only, (citing Kluber Sec. 66, Martin's Précis, Sec. 101) or by Treaty, is demanded, before it is called on to act, must have reasonable *prima facie* evidence of the guilt of the party, submitted to it, as well as the demand of the Executive authority." And again vol. 8, 215 page, in another opinion of the same, he says: "But to justify the commencement of proceeding in extradition it must appear that the criminal acts charged were committed within the territorial jurisdiction of the demanding Government."

But suppose the documents contain a charge against these prisoners, where do we find it alleged in them that the offence charged was committed within the jurisdiction of the United States of America?

The crime stated is Piracy.

In its primary and general signification, this indicates an offence against the law of nations, justiciable wherever the offender may be found. In the codes of different countries it has been arbitrarily adopted as a term applicable to offences against the Municipal Laws of such countries, or as expressed by the Commissioners in England in their report on the criminal law: "by Statutes passed at various times and still in force many artificial offences have been created which are to be deemed to amount to piracy." All such offences would be cognizable only by tribunals having jurisdiction either territorially or over the person of the offender. If it

KEN ROSSIGNOL

was intended in this case to be used in its limited or artificial sense, should not the requisition have shown it, to enable the Governor so to state it in his Warrant; otherwise how could the Justices or Officers, without knowing whether it was such an offence as would be cognizable in our Courts possibly be able to enquire into the sufficiency of the evidence according to the laws of this Province?

If it was intended to use the term, as I think it must be taken to have been in its general sense, then the question has been raised whether inasmuch as it was not alleged that any of these parties had been in the United States since the acts on the high seas complained of were committed, but the contrary was admitted on both sides, how can the offence be considered as committed within the jurisdiction of the United States?

The object of the Treaty is to be found in one of its recitals, which is: "Whereas it is found expedient for the better administration of justice and the prevention of crime within the territories and jurisdiction of the two parties respectively, that persons committing the crimes hereinafter enumerated, and being fugitives from justice, should, under certain circumstances, be reciprocally delivered up."

It is well known that the principles of the Common Law pervade the jurisprudence of both Great Britain and the United States, and by the Common Law, crimes are unquestionably considered local, cognizable and punishable exclusively in the country were they are committed ; and it was doubtless to prevent the failure of Justice that would necessarily result from offenders in one country seeking refuge in the other and there being amenable to no punishment, that this Treaty was entered into; and it is not difficult to understand how the crime of Piracy, in its general sense, might come within

138

the operation of the Treaty when a pirate having gone into one or other of the countries and so made himself amenable to its courts and had been there legally charged with the offence had fled or been subsequently found within the territory of the other, that in such a case the country where he was first found might claim jurisdiction over the crime and the person so charged. But I have great difficulty and am as yet unable to arrive at the conclusion that, when the pirate has never after committing the offence entered the country of one of the contracting parties but is found in the territory of the other, the Government of the former can assume jurisdiction over the offence and person, and require him to be given up, and so denude the latter country of its clear jurisdiction in the matter.

I cannot, as at present advised, think it was intended by this Treaty to raise such a conflict of jurisdiction and authority, but that the word piracy was intended to apply to piracy in its municipal acceptation, or if to piracy against the law of nations then to the exceptional case I have above supposed; but assuming the offence as alleged to be one within the Treaty, and the Requisition to be sufficient,

I proceed to consider the next objection.

Had Mr. Gilbert, either as Police Magistrate or a Justice of the Peace, authority to examine touching the truth of the charge?

The terms of the Statute are that the Warrant of the Governor shall "require all Justices of the Peace and other Magistrates and officers of Justice within their several jurisdictions to govern themselves accordingly and to aid in apprehending,—and thereupon it shall be lawful for any Justice of the Peace or other persons, having power to commit for trial persons accused of crimes against the laws of that part of Her Majesty's Dominions in which such supposed offenders shall be found, to examine upon oath."

The words of the Statute differ from the Treaty.

The words of the Treaty are "Judges and other Magistrates." I am bound to think this alteration advisedly made, and I find it difficult to conceive any other reason than to preserve consistency in the administration of Justice.

In the Treaty nothing is said as to the jurisdiction of the Justices and other Magistrates. In the Statute the Governor can only require Justices of the Peace and other Magistrates and officers of Justice to act within their several jurisdictions; beyond their jurisdiction then they cannot act. But the Statute says, it shall be lawful for any Justice of the Peace or other person having power to commit for trial persons accused of crime,—that is, I am inclined to think, when accused of crimes in the United States over which the officers respectively have jurisdiction to commit if committed in this Province.

Then in such cases they should examine on oath, and if the evidence would justify their committal here, issue their Warrant; and an insertion of the words "or other persons having power to commit for trial" would seem unnecessary if Justices of the Peace and other Magistrates could act in all cases.

As at present advised I am disposed to read the terms "in their several jurisdictions" in their broad signification.

I think it more consistent with the scope of the Statute and the duties to be performed that they should be considered as applying to their judicial as well as their territorial jurisdiction, it being, I think, unreasonable to
140

suppose that a Justice of the Peace, who cannot receive an information on a charge of piracy, or examine into the truth of such charge if cognizable in this Province, should, if committed in the United States, determine on the sufficiency of the evidence according to the laws of this Province if the crime was committed here; or in like manner that the Commissioners authorized solely to receive information and commit for trial in cases of offences on the high seas, should deal with crimes over which if committed in this Province they have no jurisdiction.

From this construction no possible difficulty can arise, because for every crime named in the Statute we have either the Justices of the Peace or other persons having power to commit for trial; so that in this case when it appeared by His Excellency's Warrant that the crime charged was Piracy.

Mr. Gilbert, whether as Police Magistrate or Justice of the Peace, not having jurisdiction over such an offence and no power to commit for trial a person charged with Piracy, could have referred the matter to the Judge of the Court of Vice Admiralty, or some other one of the Commissioners having authority over that offence and power to commit for trial persons charged therewith.

To confine the Magistrate and officers to their respective jurisdictions is in my opinion, in no respect to conflict with any clause in the Treaty but in harmony with it, and in furtherance of a proper and discreet execution of its stipulations.*

But assuming the Requisition right and that the Magistrate had jurisdiction, we must consider the third Point.

The question here raised was argued as if I was sitting in the character of a Court of Review or Error on the decision of the Magistrate on the facts proved before him. Such, I think, is not the case.

The duty of determining on the sufficiency of the evidence is cast on the Magistrate or other officers. He is the person to be satisfied that the evidence justifies the apprehension and committal for trial of the persons accused. The amount and value of that evidence is for his determination.

A Judge of the Supreme Court might think the evidence of guilt strong and of innocency weak, or *vice versa,* but the law has vested the Magistrate with the power of weighing and deciding on the effect of the evidence, and it is the result on his mind that is to determine its sufficiency or insufficiency.

It is a judicial discretion, with which he is vested, which, I think, is not open to question on *Habeas Corpus,* and cannot be taken from him and assumed by a Judge of the Supreme Court.

If it was manifestly apparent that the evidence showed that no offence had been committed or that the party was unquestionably innocent and therefore there was really no matter of fact or law to be tried, no matter in which the Magistrate could exercise a discretion or judgment, then the case would be very different; but is such the case before us?

That the vessel was seized and by force taken from the Captain and crew on the high seas is not disputed. Unanswered this is *a. prima facie* case of Piracy, and the burthen is cast on the accused of justifying this apparently wrongful act.

The justification set up is that hostilities were existing between the United States and the Confederate States of America, and this seizure was made under a

Commission from, or by authority and on behalf of the Confederate States, and that therefore it was an act of legitimate warfare and not of a piratical character.

This, on the other hand, is denied, and it is alleged that the claim to act under the authority of the Confederate States is mere pretense and color to disguise and cover an illegal depredation.

The object of privateering in general is not, as Mr. Kent observes fame or chivalric warfare but plunder and profit: but at the present day the rights of private armed vessels and private belligerents cannot be doubted.

Unless restrained by Treaty stipulations the right to commission private armed vessels is, by the laws of nations, esteemed a legitimate means of destroying the commerce of an enemy, and captures made by private armed vessels of one belligerent, even without a Commission, though not in self-defense, are not regarded as piratical either by their own Government or by the other belligerent State.

It does not indeed vest the enemy's property thus seized in the captors, but the seizure would be declared a prize of war to the Government of the captors ; and it is equally true that neutrals taking commission as privateers and acting on them are likewise free from the imputation of Piracy.

They may make themselves amenable for the violation of the laws of their own country, and may denude themselves of the right to claim her protection to shield them from the consequences of their acts, but they cannot be dealt with by the belligerent against whom they are acting as pirates.

But as neutrals they stand in a very different position from belligerents. Belligerents, we have seen, may make captures without commissions. Neutrals can only protect themselves by commissions from, or by acting under authority of the belligerent Government, or on board commissioned vessels, or under duly authorized officers. They cannot, without any commission or authority, fit out in a neutral country a hostile expedition against a power at peace with such country, and, under pretense of acting in The Imperial Statute 12 and 13 Vic. c. 96, passed in 1819 "to provide for the prosecution and trial, in Her Majesty's Colonies, of offences committed within the jurisdiction of the Admiralty" and giving Colonial Magistrates jurisdiction in such cases, was not cited before the Police Magistrate, nor brought to His Honor Mr. Justice Ritchie's notice in the argument in this case. It would appear to affect so much of His Honor's decision as relates to the jurisdiction of the Police Magistrate of Saint John in cases of piracy, without however affecting the conclusion finally arrived at; that being based on defects in the requisition and other proceedings, and the construction of the Imperial Statute 6 and 7 Vic. e. 76, as well as the want of jurisdiction in the Magistrate.—*Reporter.*
the name of, or on the behalf, of a belligerent power, commit acts on the high seas that would, unless protected by belligerent rights, be acts of Piracy, and not be held responsible criminally for such acts.

And therefore it behooves persons not belligerents but subjects of a neutral power engaging in acts of hostility, if they wish to escape the imputation of criminality, to be well assured when they depredate on the shipping of a nation at peace with the one to whom they owe allegiance and in opposition to the municipal laws and neutral policy of their own Government, and in
144

direct defiance of the express Proclamation of their Sovereign, that they are acting under the authority of a commission which will bear the test of a strict legal scrutiny. In the present case, can it be said that this was made out so clearly and unequivocally that there was nothing for the Magistrate to deliberate on—nothing for a Superior Court or Jury to try?

Without expressing the slightest opinion of the guilt or innocence of the parties, or the probable result of a trial either before a judicial tribunal in this Province or in the United States, it will only be necessary to refer generally to the evidence on behalf of the prisoners to show that the case is by no means so entirely free from doubt or question as their Counsel assumed.

Instead of showing that they were acting under a regular commission, or were belligerents themselves, or that the expedition proceeded from the Confederate States of America, it appears, so far as there is evidence of the nationality of the parties engaged, that they were British subjects, that the plot to seize the vessel was concocted in this City, that the commission under which they claim to act was not directed to any of the persons engaged in this capture, nor were any of them named in it, nor did it relate in any way to seizure under circumstances such as the present—that it was a commission dated 27th Oct., 1863, whereby the vessel "*Retribution*," Thomas B. Power, Commander, was authorized to act as a private armed vessel for the Confederate States on the high seas against the United States, on the back of which commission is an endorsement dated 21st Nov., 1862, signed Thomas B.

Power, whereby he transfers the command of the schooner *Retribution* to John Parker.

The commission is proved by proof of the signature of Jefferson Davis, President of the Confederate States and of the Seal of the Confederate States attached thereto; but the endorsement is proved by the slightest evidence of the hand-writing of the subscribing witness.

There is no evidence of who this John Parker was. It was proved that at Nassau a Nova Scotian named Vernon G. Locke, who had been residing for the last twenty years in the United States, and whose family is now living at Fayetteville, was last summer in the month of May at Nassau, in command of the "*Retribution*" and that he was there received and recognized as her Captain, under the name of John Parker.

Whether he was really the John Parker named on the back of the commission, or assumed that name with a view of representing that person was not shown, except as an inference might be drawn from the facts one way or other.

This commission was produced at the Lower Cove meetings by Locke *alias* Parker, but there is not a particle of evidence as to the whereabouts of the "*Retribution*" at that time or since, or that he was then Captain of her.

In fact the only evidence of her at all was her being at Nassau in May last summer.

Whether she was in existence or not, or, if in existence, where she was, or under whose command when this expedition was planned and executed, did not appear; nor was there any evidence to show that any of the parties engaged in the capture had ever been on board the "*Retribution*" or in any way connected with her. On the contrary, Braine, who would appear to have been in charge of the capturing party, described himself on board the "*Chesapeake*", and was addressed by the

146

title of Colonel Locke alias Parker, did not proceed on the expedition, (though he boarded her subsequently off Grand Manan and took the command,).

But he addressed an order to Lieut. Commanding John Clibbon Braine, "requiring him to proceed to New York with 1st Lieutenant H. A. Parr, 2nd Lieutenant David Collins, Sailing Master Tom Sayers, one Engineer and crew of 22 men; engage passage on board the steamer, using his own discretion as to time and place of capture, to act towards the crew and passengers in accordance with President's instructions, and as circumstances permit, bring his prize to Grand Manan for further orders.

This is signed John Parker, Captain C. S. Privateer "*Retribution*". There is no evidence of what these parties were officers, or how or by whom they were appointed, with the exception of David Collins, and he appears to have got his commission of second Lieutenant from John Parker. It is in these words:

To David Collins.

Reposing confidence in your zeal and ability, I do hereby authorize and commission you to hold and assume the rank of 2nd Lieutenant, and this shall be your authority for any act, under order from me, against the Government of the United States, or against the citizens of the United States, or against the property of either, by sea or by land, during the continuance of hostilities now existing. This commission to bear date from the 1st December, A. D., 1863.

(Signed) JOHN PARKER.

Had this commission been from Jefferson Davis it might have been easily understood and possibly free from question; but issued by a British subject to a British subject, in the Queen's Dominions, it is certainly a proceeding, to say the least of it, novel in its character and fairly challenging investigation. It is true, evidence was offered of military men attached to the Confederate Army showing that in operations on land officers commissioned to discharge a particular duty had, by the practice of the Confederate service, authority to appoint others under them to act as officers to carry out such duty, and that such was a recognized custom of the service.

But the practice pursued by officers unquestionably in the service of the Confederate States in the field, actually engaged in the war of the hostile territories, is not quite conclusive as to British subjects and British territory.

But be all this as it may, can it be deemed that the proceeding, if justifiable, was not, in many of its features, most irregular, and the *prima facie* case before the Magistrate being on the one hand clear, and the alleged justification presenting the irregularities and peculiarities, it did, and being open to so much question, can the Justice be fairly said to have exceeded his discretion if the result at which he arrived decided that the evidence was such as would justify their apprehension and committal for trial had the alleged crime been committed here, leaving the prisoners to substantiate their defense before a competent Court where the legal points could be properly determined.

And where the questions of intent and of fact or inference would be submitted to and determined by Jury.

As at present advised I cannot say that, in this particular, the Magistrate arrived at a wrong conclusion, nor do I think the Magistrate did wrong in refusing to go behind the Governor's warrant and determine on the sufficiency of the Requisition to His Excellency.

Over that matter, I think, the Statute gives the Justice no jurisdiction or authority.

Before leaving this branch of the case I cannot refrain from expressing my deep regret that any inhabitants of New Brunswick, being British subjects, should have been seduced from their clear duty to their Sovereign, and have availed themselves of the hospitality of a friendly power by going into its territory and obtaining a passage from one of its ports, on board one of its ships, and, by a stratagem possibly justifiable by the usages of war in a belligerent, have risen against an unarmed crew peaceably engaged in their lawful calling, and despoiled them of the property under their charge.

That too with an amount of violence resulting in the death of one of the crew, which, under the evidence in this case, would not seem to have been necessary for the accomplishment of the end sought to be attained— an example, I may be permitted to add, I earnestly trust will not be followed by any of Her Majesty's loyal subjects in this Province.

As to the 4th objection.

The Commitment first sets out, as we have seen, the Warrant of His Excellency, which alleges the parties to be charged upon the oaths of Isaac Willett and Daniel Henderson, with having committed the crimes of Piracy and Murder on the high seas within the jurisdiction of the United States of America, on the 7th December, then instant. Now where are these: averments obtained by the legal adviser of the Governor, who I presume, drafted the Warrant?

Reverting to what has been said as to the Requisition, not a word is alleged by the Consul of this crime of Murder, and not a statement made by him that either Piracy or Murder had been committed within the jurisdiction of the United States.

No doubt, the legal gentleman who drew the Warrant felt the difficulty of the want of a distinct charge, and the absolute necessity of the averment that the crime was committed within the United States of America; but as there was neither of these particulars in either of the letters of the Consul, he no doubt from necessity, resorted to the affidavit transmitted therewith of Willett and Henderson and from the facts stated by them transformed an affidavit intended, as the Consul says, "to be presented to His Excellency, in case he requires evidence of the criminality of the persons charged with the crime of Piracy before issuing the Warrant for having them brought to trial," into a charge by Willett and Henderson of Piracy and Murder.

The valuelessness of this document, either as a charge or verification, I have already shown; but where the allegation that the alleged offences were committed within the jurisdiction of the United States was obtained.

I am at a loss to conceive, for neither the Consul nor Willett nor Henderson say anything about it, unless it was assumed that as there could not be a Requisition for an offence unless so committed, the offence alleged must necessarily have been committed within the necessary jurisdiction.

Again, this Warrant does not allege that the Requisition was made by the authority of the United States but on behalf of the United States, by no means convertible terms, though it is true this allegation is preceded by the averment that in pursuance of and in accordance with the said Treaty and Act, Requisition has been made.

With these exceptions the Warrant of His Excellency appears to be in strict conformity with the Statute. Mr. Gilbert's Warrant then, as we have seen, proceeds to recite that on receipt of this Warrant he examined Isaac Willett under oath touching the truth of the charges set forth in said Warrant and upon the evidence of the said Willett, on the 25th of December, issued his Warrant for the apprehension of the persons upon the said charges: and on reference to this examination I find it is headed: "The complaint of Isaac Willett, taken and sworn to this 25th day of Dec., 1863, before me H. T. Gilbert, acting under a Warrant under the hand and seal of the Hon. A. H. Gordon, The said Isaac Willett being duly sworn".

It then details with particularity the circumstances of the capture and alleges facts not before anywhere stated, namely, the registry of the vessel in the United States of America, that the vessel at the time of capture was on the high seas about 20 miles N. N. E. of Cape Cod in the United States of America, and it avers a malicious, willful, felonious and piratical assault on, and putting in bodily fear and danger of their lives, the Captain and mariners, and the malicious, felonious and piratical taking possession of the vessel and cargo ; and that they did then and there willfully, maliciously and feloniously and violently steal take and carry away the said cargo ; and that they did with a pistol loaded with powder and leaden bullet shoot and feloniously, maliciously, willfully and piratically kill and murder one Orin Schaffer, the

151

second engineer; and in the same language and manner shot at and wounded in the right knee one Charles Johnson, chief mate ; and in the same language and manner shot and wounded in the chin James Johnson, chief engineer.

Now, with all respect for the Police Magistrate, I think this was not the proper mode of proceeding under the Statute. When he received the Governor's Warrant, assuming he had jurisdiction to act under it, he should have taken no fresh complaint. He should have embodied nothing in the form of a complaint or charge against the prisoners but what was contained in the Warrant of the Governor; and as this was his sole authority to act, he should have confined himself strictly within its requirements, which was simply in the first instance to aid in apprehending the persons accused which he should have done by issuing his Warrant reciting the Governor's Warrant, the charge therein contained against the prisoners, the requirement imposed on him thereby, and commanding the apprehension of the persons named therein, and should not have received a new complaint or introduced new charges or new matter against the accused. The correctness of this view will, I think, be confirmed by reference to the Imperial Act 8 and 9 Victoria, Chap. 120. passed 8th August, 1845, and the forms there given.

Having so examined Isaac Willett, the final commitment recites that upon the evidence of the said Isaac Willett, and in pursuance of the Act of Assembly, he issued his Warrant directing the apprehension of the parties to answer, not the charges in the Governor's Warrant, but the complaint of Isaac Willett, made on oath, for having, in the words which I before mentioned, to be dealt with according to law, the said complaint having been made and taken and this Warrant having

152

been issued in pursuance of a Warrant under the hand and seal of the Governor, in which, however, I .m constrained to differ from the learned Police Magistrate, the Warrant of the Governor not authorizing the taking of such complaint nor the arresting the parties to be dealt with according to law, but in the words of the Statute to be delivered up to justice according, and had an application been made to discharge the prisoners while detained under this Warrant.

I do not see how it could have been successfully resisted, Besset's case, C, Q. B., 481, being a direct authority against it on one point. That was the first decision under the French convention Act 6 and 7 Vic, Chap. 75, which is in the same words as the American Treaty Act we are now considering. The Warrant of the Lord Mayor there set out that the Constable should convey and deliver into custody the body of J. B. being charged before him, for that the said J. B. is accused of having committed in France the crime of Fraudulent Bankruptcy as appears by the Warrant of Arrest issued by a competent Judge in France and duly authenticated before me, and as also appears by the Warrant of one of Her Majesty's principal Secretaries of State requiring me to take cognizance of such crime. It then avers proof of the crimes and the Warrant commits the prisoner until he should be discharged by due course of law, which is the effect under this commitment under the words, to be dealt with according to law.

But the Court held the Warrant bad upon the grounds that as the commitment were under a special statutory authority, the terms of the commitment must be special and exactly pursue that authority, acting on

153

and recognizing the authority of Mash's case, 2 Win. Bl. 806, where it is laid down that the true distinction is that when a man is committed for any crime, either at Common Law or created by Act of Parliament, for which he is punishable by indictment, then he is to be committed until discharged by due course of law, but when it is in pursuance of a special authority the terms of the commitment must be special and exactly pursue that authority.

The commitment then proceeds to aver that the prisoners having been brought before the Justice under the Warrant, and he having proceeded to the investigation of the charge of Piracy charged against them, and upon examination of the witnesses under oath touching the offence of Piracy, and upon the evidence before him, so under oath, he did, under the Act of Parliament, require and command the said Constable to convey the prisoners to the Common Jail, and deliver each of them to the Keeper thereof upon the charge of Piracy, for that they having on the 7th day of December, and then proceeds to recapitulate the particulars of the charge in the complaint made before him by Isaac Willett, omitting the felonious, murder and shooting, there to remain till delivered pursuant to the Requisition aforesaid. On referring to the examinations themselves, we find the charge on which the examination proceeded was of an offence which it alleges took place on the high seas, about 20 miles N. N. East of Cape Cod, in the United States of America, and within the jurisdiction of the United States of America, and the Circuit Courts thereof, against the laws of the United States of America, and the statutes of the United Kingdom of Great Britain and Ireland. So we see that at every stage of these proceedings the charge assumes a different phase.

In the first instance the Consul simply presents the complaint as that certain persons were believed to be guilty of the crime of Piracy. The Governor's Warrant puts it as a charge of Piracy and murder, on the high seas, within the jurisdiction of the United States of America, on the complaint of Willett and Henderson.

The complaint before the Police Magistrate is the complaint of Willett alone, and alleges the crimes of **Piracy and Murder** in the United States of America, and adds the felonious shooting and wounding of engineer and mate, and felonious stealing of the cargo.

And on the examination before Mr. Gilbert there is the addition of the crime being within the jurisdiction of the Circuit Courts of the United States, and being contrary to the laws of the United States of America and the statutes of Great Britain and Ireland.

But independent of these discrepancies, which would seem to me difficult to reconcile, or on legal principles to account for, there is, to my mind, a still more substantial objection to this warrant.

This is the final commitment of the accused to Jail, there to remain until delivered pursuant to the Requisition. But after examination of the witnesses, and before the committal, there was something to be done, an all-important duty to be discharged, which I cannot discover from the Warrant or from any of the proceedings before me, and I can look to nothing else, to have been performed, and which, if done, I think should clearly, unequivocally and unambiguously appear on the face of the Warrant, which it manifestly docs not; and that is, that alter hearing and considering the evidence, the Justice determined and adjudicated that he deemed the same sufficient according to the laws of this Province to justify the apprehension and committal for trial of the prisoners, if the crime had been committed within this Province.

Without such adjudication, the Warrant of commitment could not issue, and without such an adjudication appearing on the face of it when issued, I think the Warrant bad, there being without it a want of jurisdiction shown to issue the Warrant, or perhaps rather a want of jurisdiction to sustain it; and this view is confirmed by reference to 8 & 9 Vic., chap. 20, before referred to, for even there where a statutory form is given to be used by the Police Magistrate of the Metropolis, the adjudication is set forth.

The form is given thus; "Be it remembered that on A. B. is brought before me, J. P. &. and is charged before me for that he, the said A. B., on &c., within the jurisdiction of the United States of America did (here state the offence); and forasmuch as it has been shown to me upon such evidence as by law is sufficient to justify the committal to Jail of the said A. B. pursuant to an Act passed in the 7th year of the Reign of her Majesty entitled, that the said A. B. is guilty of the said offence, this is therefore to command."

The cases to be found bearing on this point lay down the principle very clearly, some of which I will quote. *In re* Peerless 1 Q. B.152. This was a Warrant setting forth a conviction—Denman C. J. says "The Magistrate having no jurisdiction except by the express Statutory enactment, the offence is not here described sufficiently to show jurisdiction." Per Littledale J. "I do not say that this may not be a good conviction upon which a good Warrant might be framed, but I think this Warrant clearly bad for not showing jurisdiction.

In what way it is that Justices have jurisdiction, ought to appear by the Warrant. I found myself on Lord Tenterden's Judgment in Kite & Lane's case, 1 B., and C. 101."

And Coleridge J. says; "By a legal Warrant, I mean a Warrant which upon the face of it shows a right to detain, and that right cannot exist unless there is jurisdiction in the Magistrates. To deny that this must appear upon the face of the proceedings is to call in question one of the most important rules of the Criminal Law".

In Kite & Lane's case referred to. Abbot C. J. says: "It is a first principle as to all acts done by Magistrates that the jurisdiction should appear on the face of their proceedings."

And Best J. says "It is a settled principle that penal Statutes, and such as create new jurisdiction shall receive a strict construction. Nash's case 4th B. and A. 295, was the case of a warrant issued under the 57th George 3d, Cap. 87 Sec. 0, by which Act, in case any person, found on board a vessel liable to forfeiture under 45 George 3, Cap. 121 be fit and able to serve his Majesty in his naval service, he shall upon such proof as by the said Act of the 45th year aforesaid, is required, be committed by such Justice to prison, to answer such information and abide such judgment.

Abbot C. J. says:—"This .Act of Parliament of the 57th year of George 3, Cap. 87, is one highly beneficial in preventing frauds upon the revenue, but at the same time, inasmuch as it trenches very strongly on the liberty of the subject, we must take care that its provisions are strictly pursued."

157

And again; "these circumstances stated in the introductory part of this return seem to me quite sufficient to warrant this commitment, and if it had been stated upon due proof of the matters before mentioned the prisoner was committed, I should have thought it sufficient."

And Per Holroyd, J. "The power of the Magistrate to commit depends on the proof before him, and the Rule is, that where a limited authority is given it must be shown to have been strictly pursued."

And in Christy v. Unwin, 11 Ad. and El. 377, where the validity of an order made by the Lord Chancellor under 6th George 4th, Chap. 16, Sec. 18, was questioned, it was held that the order must show on the face of it whatever was necessary to give jurisdiction.

And Coleridge, J. says:— "We cannot intend for or against the order but must decide according to the words. However high the authority may be where a statutory power is exercised, the person who acts must take care to bring himself within the terms of the Statute.

Whether the order he made by the Lord Chancellor or by a Justice of the Peace, the facts which give the authority must be stated." This case is, I believe, the first under the Treaty and Act of Parliament **that** has called for judicial investigation in this Province, and as points of a novel, certainly of a peculiar, and I may say of a delicate, certainly of an important character have been raised, I have endeavored to give the case the most careful consideration, and in view of the possibility of this decision becoming the subject of discussion in other quarters, I have, to prevent misapprehension, felt it right, though at the risk of subjecting myself to the charge of unnecessary prolixity, to place on the face of my judgment, at length, the documents and facts necessary to enable all interested in the matter who have not access to the papers before me, or who may not have heard the arguments, correctly to understand the points raised and the reasons for the conclusion at which I have arrived.

In the prompt manner in which His Excellency the Lieut. Governor granted his Warrant, and in the determination of the Police Magistrate on the fads of the case, the Government of the United States cannot fail, I think, to discern the determination of the Queen's Representative and Her subordinate officers faithfully and honorably to carry out the Treaty entered into between the respective Governments of the United States and Great Britain ; and the present decision, the result of my own judicial convictions, being, I believe, in conformity with the legal authorities of the United States, individually I might hope it would commend itself to the United States Government; but whomsoever it may please op displease must be to me, judicially, a matter of indifference. The only duty I have to discharge is to my Sovereign, to the people of this Province, and to my own conscience.

That duty is, faithfully, to the best of my humble abilities, impartially, to declare the Law as I believe it to be, wholly regardless of consequences.

This I have honestly endeavored to do, and the result of my judgment is, that for the reasons set forth, the proceedings before me, and the Warrant of commitment, returned to me by the Sheriff of the City and County of Saint John, do not justify the detention in custody of the prisoners, whose imprisonment I therefore declare illegal; and I do by this my order require the immediate discharge from prison of the said David Collins, James McKinney and Linus Seely, under the said Warrant and commitment; and as it appears to me that the Sheriff of the City and County of Saint John, the keeper of the Jail of the said City and County, acted upon the Warrant or commitment of the said H. T. Gilbert, according to the requirements of the same, without malice or evil intent, I do, by virtue of the power conferred on me by the Act of Assembly, exempt the said keeper of the said Jail from all civil suits which may be brought against him for or by reason of having acted on the said Warrant or commitment.

APPENDIX

A.

REQUISITIONS OF THE UNITED STATES CONSUL.

Saint John, N. B., Dec. 22nd, 1863.

HON. S. L. TILLEY, *Provincial Secretary*

Sir:—I beg leave to transmit the depositions of the Captain and second Mate of the Steamer Chesapeake., to be presented to his Excellency, in case he requires evidence of the criminality of the persons charged with the crime of Piracy, before issuing the warrant for having them brought to Trial. It is to be sincerely hoped that no obstacles will be thrown in the way of bringing those charged with so grave an offence to justice.

We had believed until this late hour that a requisition before the Executive would not have been required in the first instance.

Yours truly,

(Signed) J. Q. HOWARD, U. S. Consul.
UNITED STATES CONSULATE,
St. John, New Brunswick, December 22, 1863.
HON. S. L. TILLEY, *Provincial Secretary.*
SIR,—

I have the honor to address, through you, a communication to the Lieutenant Governor of the

Province, for the purpose of requesting that his Excellency will be pleased to use the authority vested in him by the Act of Parliament for giving effect to what is known as the "Ashburton Treaty" to the end that certain offenders may be apprehended aid delivered up to Justice.

You will please make known to His Excellency, that as an officer of the Government of the United States, I am authorized by the Executive Department of the Government to make a requisition upon him, as the officer administering the Government of the Province, in order that certain persons believed to be guilty of the crime of Piracy may he brought before the proper officers of Justice, so that the evidence of their guilt or innocence may be heard and considered. I have, therefore, the honor to request, that in accordance with the provisions of the said Acts of Parliament,

His Excellency will by Warrant signify that a requisition has been made for the apprehension of John C. Braine, H. C. Brooks, David Collins John Parker Locke, Robert Clifford, Linus Seely, George Robinson, Gilbert Cox, Robert Cox, H. H. Parr, and James McKinney, and require that all Justices of the Peace and other Magistrates, within the Jurisdiction of this Province, shall aid in apprehending the above named persons, accused of the crime of Piracy, for the purpose of having them brought to trial. I am sir,

Your obedient Servant,
(Signed) J. Q. HOTVAED, V. S. Consul.

I HEREBY CERTIFY that the foregoing are true copies of the original letters and requisition of J. Q. Howard, Esq., United States Consul, at the City of Saint John, and are now on file in my office,

(Signed) S. L. TILLEY, Prov. Secretary.

162

Secretary's Office, 29th January, 1864,

B.

Extract from the Treaty between Her Majesty and the United States of America, signed at Washington, August 9, 1842; commonly known as the "Ashburton Treaty."

ARTICLE X.

"It is agreed that Her Britannic Majesty and the United States shall, upon mutual requisitions by them or their ministers, officers, or authorities, respectively made, deliver up to justice all persons who, being charged with the crime of murder, or assault with intent to commit murder, or piracy, or arson, or rubbery, or forgery or the utterance of forged paper, committed within the jurisdiction of either, shall seek an asylum, or shall be found within the territories of the other:— provided that this shall only be done upon such evidence of criminality as, according to the laws of the place where the fugitive or person so charged shall be found, would justify his apprehension and commitment for trial, if the crime or offence had there been committed ; and the respective Judges and other Magistrates of the two Governments shall have power, jurisdiction, and authority, upon complaint made under oath, to issue a Warrant for the apprehension of the fugitive or person so charged, that he may be brought before such Judges or other Magistrates, respectively, to the end that the evidence of criminality may be heard and considered and if, on such hearing, the evidence be deemed sufficient to sustain the charge, it shall be the duty of the examining Judge or Magistrate to certify the same to the proper executive authority, that a warrant may issue for the surrender of such fugitive. The expense of such apprehension and delivery shall be borne and defrayed by the Party who makes the requisition and receives the fugitive."

C.

6 & 7 VIC, CAP. LXX. VI.
An Act for giving effect to a Treaty between Her Majesty and the United States of-America for the apprehension of certain offenders.

WHEREAS by the Tenth Article of a Treaty between Her Majesty and the United States of America, signed at Washington on the ninth day of August in the year one thousand eight hundred and forty two, the Ratifications whereof were exchanged in London on the thirteenth day of October in the same year, it was agreed that Her Majesty and the said United States should, upon mutual Requisitions by them or their Ministers, Officers, or Authorities respectively made, deliver up to Justice all Persons who being charged with the crime of Murder, or Assault with Intent to commit Murder, or Piracy, or Arson, or Robbery, or Forgery, or the Utterance of forged Paper, committed within the jurisdiction of cither of the High Contracting Parties, should seek an asylum or should be found within the Territories of the other; provided that this should only be done upon such evidence of criminality as according to the Laws of the place where the Fugitive or Person so charged should be found would justify his Apprehension and Commitment for Trial if the Crime or Offence had been there committed, and that the respective Judges and other Magistrates of the two Governments should have Power, Jurisdiction, and authority, upon Complaint made under Oath, to issue a Warrant for the Apprehension of the Fugitive or Person so charged, so that he might be brought before such Judges or other Magistrates respectively, to the end that the Evidence of Criminality might be heard and considered, and if on such

Hearing the Evidence should be deemed sufficient to sustain the Charge it should be the duty of the examining Judge or Magistrate to certify the same to the proper executive authority, that a Warrant might issue for the Surrender of such Fugitive, and that the expense of such Apprehension and Delivery should be borne and defrayed by the party making the Requisition and receiving the Fugitive ; and it is by the Eleventh Article of the said Treaty further agreed, that the Tenth Article hereinbefore recited, should continue in force until one or other of the High Contracting Parties should signify its wish to terminate it, and no longer.

And whereas it is expedient that Provision should be made for carrying the said Agreement into effect, be it enacted by the Queen's Most Excellent Majesty by and with the advice and consent of the Lords Spiritual and Temporal, and Commons, in this present Parliament assembled, and by the authority of the same,

That in case Requisition shall at any time be made by the Authority of the said United States, in pursuance of and according to the said Treaty, for the Delivery of any Person charged with the Crime of Murder, or Assault with intent to commit Murder, or with the Crime of Piracy, or Arson, or Robbery, or Forgery, or the utterance of forged Paper, committed within the Jurisdiction of the

United States of America, who shall he found within the Territories of Her Majesty, it shall be lawful for One of Her Majesty's Principal Secretaries of State, or in Ireland for the Chief Secretary of the Lord Lieutenant of Ireland, and in any of Her Majesty's Colonies or Possessions abroad for the Officer administering the Government of any such Colony or Possession, by Warrant under his Hand and Seal to signify that such Requisition has been so made, and to require all Justices of the Peace and other Magistrates and Officers of Justice within their several Jurisdictions to govern themselves accordingly, and to aid in apprehending the Person so accused, and committing such person to Jail, for the purpose of being delivered up to Justice, according to the provisions of the said Treaty ; and thereupon it shall be lawful for any Justice of the Peace, or other Person having Power to commit for trial Persons accused of crimes against the Laws of that Part of Her Majesty's Dominions in which such supposed Offender shall he found, to examine upon Oath any Person or Persons touching the Truth of such Charge, and upon such Evidence as according to the Laws of that Part of Her Majesty's Dominions would justify the Apprehension and Committal for Trial of the Person so accused if the Crime of which he or she shall be so accused had been there committed it shall be lawful for such Justice of the Peace, or other Person having Power to commit as aforesaid, to issue his Warrant for the Apprehension of such Person, and also to commit the Person so accused to Jail, there to remain until delivered Pursuant to such Requisition as aforesaid.

"**II. Provided always, and be it enacted,** That in every such Case, Copies of the Depositions upon which the original Warrant was granted, certified under the Hand of the Person or Persons issuing such Warrant, and attested upon the Oath of the Party producing them to be true Copies of the original Depositions, may be received in Evidence of the Criminality of the Person so apprehended."

[The remaining sections of the Act are not material to the decision in this case.]

D.

WARRANT ISSUED BY THE LIEUTENANT GOVERNOR UNDER THE TREATY AND STATUTE.

NEW BRUNSWICK.

By His Excellency the Honorable

ARTHUR HAMILTON GORDON,
[SEAL.]

C. M. G., Lieutenant Governor and Commander-in-Chief of the Province of New Brunswick,

ARTHUR H. GORDON.

To all and every the Justices of the Peace and Officers of Justice within the Province of New Brunswick, Greeting:

Whereas in and by an Act of Parliament made and passed in the sixth and seventh years of the reign of Her Majesty Queen Victoria, entitled "An Act for giving effect to a Treaty between Her Majesty and the United States of America for the apprehension of certain offenders, "it is among other things enacted" that in case requisition shall at any time be made by the authority of the said United States, in pursuance of and according to the said Treaty for the delivery of any person charged with the crime of murder, or assault with intent to commit

168

murder, or with the crime of piracy, or arson, or robbery, or forgery, or the utterance of forged paper, committed within the jurisdiction of the United States of America, who shall be found within the Territories of Her Majesty, it shall be lawful for one of Her Majesty's principal Secretaries of State, or in Ireland, for the Chief Secretary of the Lord Lieutenant of Ireland, and in any of Her Majesty's Colonies or Possessions abroad, for the Officer administering the Government of any such Colony or Possession by warrant under his hand and seal to signify that such requisition has been so made, and to require all Justices of the Peace and other Magistrates and Officers of Justice within their several jurisdictions to govern themselves accordingly and to aid in apprehending the person so accused and committing such person to jail for the purpose of being delivered up to Justice according to the provisions of the said Treaty, and thereupon it shall be lawful for any Justice of the Peace or other person having power to commit for trial persons accused of crimes against the laws of that part of Her Majesty's dominions in which such supposed offender shall be found, to examine upon oath any person or persons touching the truth of such charge and upon such evidence as according to the laws of that part of Her Majesty's dominions would justify the apprehension and committal for trial of the person so accused of the crime of which he or she shall be so accused, had been there committed, it shall be lawful for such Justice of the Peace or other person having power to commit as aforesaid, to issue his warrant for the apprehension of such person, and also to commit the person so accused to jail there to remain until delivered pursuant to such requisition as aforesaid.

And whereas, in pursuance of and in accordance with the said Treaty and Act, a Requisition has been made to me, on behalf of the said United States, by J. Q. Howard, Consul of the said United States at the City of Saint John, in this Province, stating that John C. Braine, H. C. Brooks, David Collins, John Parker Locke, Robert Clifford, Linus Seely, George Robinson, Gilbert Cox, Robert Cox, H. A. Parr, and James McKinney, charged upon the oath of Isaac Willett and Daniel Henderson with having committed the crimes of Piracy and Murder on the High Seas, within the Jurisdiction of the said United States of America, on the seventh day of December instant, are, or some of them are now in the City of Saint John, within this Province, and requesting that the said John C. Braine, H. C. Brooks, David Collins, John Parker Locke, Robert Clifford, Linus Seely, George Robinson, Gilbert Cox, Robert Cox, H. A. Parr, and James McKinney, may be delivered up to Justice according to the provisions of the said Treaty. Now KNOW YE, that pursuant to this power in me vested in and by the said Act of Parliament, I do hereby, by this warrant under my hand and seal, signify that such requisition has been so made, and hereby require and command all Justices of the Peace and other Magistrates and other officers of Justice of this Province, within their several jurisdictions, to govern themselves accordingly and to aid in apprehending the said John C. Braine, H. C. Brooks, David Collins, John Parker Locke, Robert Clifford, Linus Seely. George Robinson, Gilbert Cox, Robt. Cox, H. A. Parr, and James McKinney, so accused, and committing them, the said John C, Braine, H. C Brooks, David Collins, John Parker Locke, Robert Clifford, Linus Seely, George Robinson, Gilbert Cox, Robert Cox, H. A. Parr, and James

McKinney, to Jail for the purpose of being delivered up to Justice according to the provisions of the said Treaty. - And hereof they will not fail at their peril.

Given under my hand and Seal at Fredericton, in this Province of New Brunswick, this Twenty fourth day of December, in the twenty-seventh year of Her Majesty's Reign. Anno Domini, 1863.

By His Excellency's Command,
(Signed) S. L. TILLEY.

E.

COMPLAINT OF CAPTAIN WILLETT, TAKEN BY THE POLICE MAGISTRATE OF SAINT JOHN,

the 25th December, 1863.City and County of Saint John,—to-wit:

The complaint of Isaac Willett, of the State of New York, in the United States of America, Master Mariner, now in the City of Saint John, aforesaid, taken and sworn to, this Twenty-fifth day of December, in the Year of Our Lord One Thousand Eight Hundred and Sixty-three, at the City aforesaid, before me Humphrey T. Gilbert. Esq., Police Magistrate for the City of Saint John, and one of Her Majesty's Justices of the Peace for the City and County of Saint John, acting under a warrant under the hand and seal of His Excellency the Honorable Arthur H. Gordon, Lieutenant Governor and Commander-in-Chief of the Province of New Brunswick, bearing date the twenty-fourth day of December, one thousand eight hundred and sixty-three, and made and issued in pursuance of the Act of the Imperial Parliament, entitled

171

an Act for giving effect to a Treaty between Her Majesty and the United States of America, for the apprehension of certain offenders ; such warrant directed to all and every the Justices of the Peace, and officers of Justice within the Province of New Brunswick.

The said Isaac Willett being duly sworn, says as follows: that he this deponent on the seventh day of December, one thousand eight hundred and sixty three, was Master in charge and command of the American passenger steamboat or vessel *Chesapeake*, and owned by Henry B. Cromwell, of the State of New York in the United States of America, Merchant. That the said steamboat or vessel is duly registered in pursuance of the United States laws for the registering of ships or vessels, and was so registered on the seventh day of December, instant.

That the said steamboat or vessel was of the value of the sum of sixty thousand dollars and upwards of current money of New Brunswick, and had on board a valuable cargo of the value of eighty thousand dollars and upwards of like current money, and there were at the time a number of passengers on board of the said ship or vessel. That the said vessel or steamboat left the Port of New York on the fifth day of December instant, being then duly registered as aforesaid, with the cargo of the value aforesaid on board, and a number of passengers on a voyage from said Port of New York to the Port of Portland, in the said United States, this deponent being in command of the said steamboat or vessel. That John C. Braine, H. C. Brooks, David Collins, Robert Clifford, Linus Seely, George Robinson, Gilbert Cox, Robert Cox, H. A. Parr, and James McKinney, having taken passage on board of the said steamboat or vessel, left the said Port of New York, in and on board the said steamboat or vessel, as passengers on the said voyage.

172

That the said steamboat or vessel proceeded on her said voyage, and while on the said voyage this deponent being in command of said steamboat or vessel, the said vessel then being on the high seas about twenty miles North North East of Cape Cod, in the United States of America, on the seventh day of December instant, certain passengers on board the said vessel, namely, the said John C. Braine, H. C. Brooks, David Collins, Robert Clifford, Linus Seely, George Robinson, Gilbert Cox, Robert Cox, H. A. Parr, and James McKinney, so being passengers on board the said steamboat or vessel, with force and arms, on the high seas, in and on board the said steamboat or vessel called the *Chesapeake*, in a certain place upon the high seas, distant about twenty-miles from Cape Cod aforesaid then being, in and upon this deponent and upon others the mariners then navigating the said vessel upon the said voyage, maliciously, willfully, feloniously, and piratically, did make an assault and this deponent and others, the said mariners, then and there piratically, feloniously', willfully, and maliciously, did put in bodily fear and danger of their lives on the high seas aforesaid, and then and there maliciously, willfully, feloniously and piratically took possession of the said steamboat or vessel and the cargo thereof; the said steamboat or vessel being under the charge and command of this deponent, and there and then with force and arms look the said steamboat or vessel, and cargo of said vessel, from the care and custody of this deponent and the said mariners, against the will of this deponent and the said mariners and then and there with force and arms upon the high seas aforesaid in the place aforesaid and within the

173

Jurisdiction of the United States of America, **piratically, willfully, maliciously, and feloniously and violently did steal, take, and carry away the said vessel and cargo**, and the said named persons did then and there with a pistol loaded with powder and leaden bullets shoot at, and **feloniously', maliciously, willfully, and piratically, kill and murder one Orin Schaffer**, the second engineer, he being then a hand employed in and on board the said steamboat or vessel on the voyage aforesaid, and the said named persons having so taken possession of the said steamboat or vessel, put this deponent and others the crew of said vessel from the steamboat or vessel into and on board a pilot boat and the said named persons also then and there willfully, feloniously, maliciously, and piratically, with a pistol loaded with powder and leaden bullets shot at and wounded in the right knee and left arm one Charles Johnston, he the said Charles Johnston, then and there being chief mate of the said steamboat or vessel, and also then and there with a pistol loaded with powder and leaden bullets willfully, feloniously, maliciously, and piratically shot at and wounded in the chin, one James Johnston, he, the said James Johnston, then and there being Chief Engineer in and on board the said vessel, and this deponent further says that the said named persons having so taken possession of the said steamboat or vessel, they the said named persons proceeded from the said place where the said offences were committed, to and up the Bay of Fundy, and that having proceeded to a place on the high seas about fifteen miles below Dipper Harbor, in the Province of New Brunswick, one John Parker Locke came to the said steamboat or vessel and boarded her, and immediately took charge and command of the said steamboat or vessel and cargo, against the will of deponent and others the mariners of the said ship or vessel. That until the said
174

John Parker Locke came on board of the said vessel, the said John C. Braine appeared to have Command of the persons who so piratically took possession of the said ship or vessel as aforesaid, and this deponent further says that he verily believes the said John C. Braine is now in the City of Saint John, in the Province of New Brunswick.

(Signed) ISAAC WILLETT.

Sworn at the City of Saint John, in the City and County of Saint John, this 25th day of December, A. D., 1863, before me.

(Signed) H. T. GILBERT, *P. M. and J. P.*

F.

WARRANT FOR THE APPREHENSION OF THE PRISONERS, ISSUED BY THE POLICE MAGISTRATE.

To any Constable or Peace Officer of the City, or City and County of Saint John.

Apprehend John C. Braine, H. C. Brooks, David Collins, Robert Clifford, Linus Seely, George Robinson, Gilbert Cox, Robert Cox, H. A. Parr, and James McKinney, and bring them before me or some other Justice at the Police Office in the City of Saint John, to answer the complaint of Isaac Willett, of the State of New York, in the United States of America, Master Mariner, made on oath for having on the Seventh day of December, in the Year of Our Lord One Thousand Eight Hundred and Sixty-three, on the high seas, about twenty miles North North East of Cape Cod, in the United States of America, on the Seventh day of December aforesaid, with force and arms,

175

maliciously, willfully, feloniously, and piratically, made an assault upon the said Isaac Willett, and others the Mariners then on board, and in Charge and Command of the Steamboat or Vessel named the Chesapeake, the said Vessel being a Vessel belonging to one Henry B. Cromwell, a Citizen of the United States of America, and being of the value of sixty thousand dollars of lawful money of New Brunswick, and having on board a Cargo of the value of eighty thousand dollars of like lawful money, and the said Vessel being then on a Voyage from the Port of New York, in the United States of America, to the Port of Portland, in the said United States of America, and having then and there piratically, feloniously, willfully, and maliciously put the said Isaac Willett and others the Crew of the said Vessel, in fear and danger of their lives on the high seas aforesaid, and having then and there maliciously, willfully, feloniously, and piratically taken possession of the said Vessel and the Cargo thereof, and with having then and there feloniously, willfully, maliciously, and piratically stolen and taken the said Vessel and Cargo upon the high seas aforesaid, and also for having at the time and place aforesaid, feloniously, willfully, maliciously, and piratically upon the high seas aforesaid, killed and murdered one Orin Schaffer, in and on board the said Vessel on the said Voyage, and also for having at the time and place aforesaid, with force and arms, feloniously, willfully, maliciously, and piratically assaulted and wounded one Charles Johnston, and also for having at the time and place aforesaid, feloniously, willfully, maliciously, and piratically assaulted and wounded one James Johnston, and to be dealt with according to Law. The said complaint having been made and taken, and this Warrant having been issued in pursuance of a Warrant under the hand and seal of His Excellency The Honorable

Arthur H. Gordon, Lieutenant Governor, and Commander in Chief of the Province of New Brunswick, bearing date the Twenty-fourth day of December,

One Thousand Eight Hundred and Sixty-three, and made and issued in pursuance of the Act of the Imperial Parliament, entitled, an Act for giving effect to a treaty between Her Majesty and the United States of America, for the apprehension of certain offenders.

Dated this 25th day of December, in the Year of Our Lord One Thousand Eight Hundred and Sixty-three, and given under my hand and seal on the said date.

(Signed) H. T. GILBEKT, [L. B.]
Pol. Mag. & Jus, of the Peace.

G.

COMMISSION OF THE C. S. PRIVATEER
RETRIBUTION AND TRANSFERTO CAPTAIN PARKER.

JEFFERSON DAVIS,
President of the Confederate States of America.

To all who shall see these presents,—Greeting:

Know ye, that by virtue of the power vested in me by law, I have commissioned and do hereby commission, have authorized and do hereby authorize the vessel called the *Retribution* (more particularly described in the Schedule hereunto annexed,) whereof Thomas B. Power is Commander, to act as a private armed vessel in the service of the Confederate States, on the high seas, against the United States of America, their ships, vessels, goods and effects, and those of their citizens, during the

177

pendency of the war now existing between the said Confederate States and the said United States.

This commission to continue in force until revoked by the President of the Confederate States for the time being.

Given under my hand and the Seal of the Confederate States at Richmond this 27th day of October, A. D., 1863.

By the President, (Signed) JEFFERSON DAVIS.
(Signed) J. P. BENJAMIN, Secretary of State.

Schedule of description of the vessel.
Name—*Retribution*.
Tonnage—150.
Armament—3 guns.
No. of Crew—30.
(Endorsed.)
State of South Carolina
District of Charleston
I hereby transfer the command of the schooner *Retribution* to John Parker Witness, ray hand and Seal, this twenty-first day of November. 1862.

Witness (Signed) THOMAS B. POWEH, (L.S.)
(Signed) W. F. COLCOCK, Collector.

H

ORDERS FROM CAPTAIN PARKER
TO LIEUT. BRAINE
ORDERS.

To Lieut. Commanding John Clibbon Braine, You are hereby ordered to proceed to the City of New York and State aforesaid with the following officers; 1st Lieut. H. A.

Parr, 2nd Lieut. David Collins, Sailing Master Tom Sayers, 1st Engineer Smith, and crew of 22men. You will upon arrival there engage passage on board the steamer and use your own discretion as to the proper time and place of capture. Your action towards crew and passengers will be strictly in accordance with the President's instructions. You will as circumstances may permit bring your prize to the Island of Grand Manan for further orders, Seal Cove Harbor if accessible.

(Signed) JOHN PARKER,
Capt. C. S. Privateer *Retribution*.
December 3nd, 1863.

COMMISSION TO DAVID COLLINS.

I.

To David Collins.

Reposing confidence in your zeal and ability, I do hereby authorize and commission you to hold and assume the rank of 2nd Lieutenant, and this shall be your authority for any act, under orders from me, against the Government of the United States, against the citizens of the United States, or against the property of either, by sea or by land, during the continuance of hostilities now existing.

This commission to bear date from the 1st day of December, A. D., 1863.

(Signed) JOHN PARKER.

HEADING OF THE EVIDENCE ETC., RETURNED BY THE POLICE MAGISTRATE BEFORE THE JUDGE.

KEN ROSSIGNOL

David Collins, James McKinney, and Linus Seely
stand charged before me, Humphrey T. Gilbert, Esquire,
Police Magistrate of the City of Saint John, and one of
Her Majesty's Justices of the Peace for the City and
County of Saint John, acting under a warrant under the
hand and seal of His Excellency The Honorable Arthur
Hamilton Gordon, C. M. G., Lieutenant Governor, and
Commander in Chief of the Province of New Brunswick,
bearing date the twenty-fourth day of December, in the
Year of Our Lord One Thousand Eight Hundred and Sixty
three and made and issued in pursuance of the Act of the
Imperial Parliament entitled, **"An Act for giving effect to
a Treaty between Her Majesty and the United States of
America, for the apprehension of certain offenders,"**
such warrant being directed to all and every the Justices
of the Peace and Officers of Justice, within the Province
of New Brunswick—For that they the said David Collins,
James McKinney, and Linus Seely, (together with John C.
Braine, H. C. Brooks, Robert Clifford, George Robinson,
Gilbert Cox, Robert Cox, and H. A. Parr, not brought up
before me for examination,) did on the seventh day of
December in the Year of Our Lord One Thousand Eight
Hundred and Sixty-three, upon the high seas, about
twenty miles North North East of Cape Cod, in the said
United States of America, and within the jurisdiction of
the said United States of America, and the Circuit Courts
thereof, then being passengers in and on board a certain
passenger and freight steamer called the *Chesapeake*,
United States of America Register, owned, belonging,
and appertaining to Henry B. Cromwell, a subject of the
said United States of America, whereof Isaac Willett, also
a subject thereof was Master, while on a voyage from
New York to Portland, in the said United States of
America, with force and arms turned pirates and the said
steam vessel and the apparel and tackle thereof of the
180

value of sixty thousand dollars of lawful money of the said United States of America and of the Province of New Brunswick, and a cargo owned by persons unknown of the value of eighty thousand dollars of like lawful money then and there being in the said steam vessel under the care and custody and in the possession of the said Isaac Willett as master of the said steam vessel, then and there upon the high seas aforesaid, within the jurisdiction aforesaid, about the distance of twenty miles North North East of Cape Cod aforesaid with force and arms from the care, custody, and possession of the said Isaac Willett and against the will of the said Isaac Willett and the crew and mariners assisting the said Isaac Willett in the navigation of the said steam vessel, piratically and feloniously did steal, take, and run away with, they the said David Collins, James McKinney and Linus Seely, being passengers on board of the said steam vessel and in and on board the same on the high seas aforesaid, against the laws of the United States of America and the Statutes of the United Kingdom of Great Britain and Ireland.

K.

RETURN, OF THE SHERIFF TO THE ORDER OF *HABEAS CORPUS.*

SUPREME COURT

I, James A. Harding, Sheriff of the City and County of Saint John, having charge of the Jail of the said City and County, do hereby certify that David Collins, James

McKinney, and Linus Seely, named in the annexed order were in the jail of the City and County of Saint John, for safe keeping, under a warrant from H. T. Gilbert, Esq., Police Magistrate, and Justice of the Peace, from the following dates:—James McKinney, from the 26th day of December last, David Collins, from the 37th day of December last, and Linus Seely, from the first day of January last past, except when ordered for examination by the said H. T. Gilbert, Police Magistrate, and Justice of the Peace, up to 11 o'clock or thereabouts, on the morning of the 24th day of February, inst., when they were taken to the office of the said H. T. Gilbert, Police Magistrate and Justice of the Peace. That they were committed to the jail of the said City and County, at mid-day of the 25th day of

February, inst., with the following, a copy of the commitment:

"City and County of Saint John, to wit;—To any Constable, or Peace Officer, of the City and County of Saint John, and to the keeper of the Gaol (Jail) thereof; you the said Constable, shall convey David Collins, of the City of Saint John, Laborer, James McKinney, of the same place. Laborer, and Linus Seely, of the same place, Laborer, charged before me, Humphrey T. Gilbert, Esq., Police Magistrate for the City of Saint John, and one of Her Majesty's Justices of the Peace for the City and County of Saint John, acting under warrant under the hand and seal of

His Excellency the Honorable Arthur Hamilton Gordon, C. M. G, Lieutenant Governor, and Commander in Chief of the Province of New Brunswick, bearing date the twenty-fourth day of December, in the Year of Our Lord One Thousand Eight Hundred and Sixty-three, and made and issued in pursuance of the Act of Imperial Parliament entitled, "An Act for giving effect to a Treaty

182

between Her. Majesty and the United States of America, for the apprehension of certain offenders," and in pursuance of and in accordance with the said Treaty' and Act, a Requisition having been made to His Excellency the Honorable .Arthur Hamilton Gordon, C. M. G., Lieutenant Governor, and Commander in Chief of the Province of New Brunswick, on behalf of the said United States of America, by James Q.

Howard, Consul of the said United States, at the City of Saint John, in the Province of New Brunswick, stating that John C. Braine, H. C. Brooks, David Collins, John Parker Locke, Robert Clifford, Linus Seely, George Robinson, Gilbert Cox, Robert Cox, H. A. Parr, and James McKinney, charged upon the oath of Isaac

Willett, and Daniel Henderson, with having committed the crimes of piracy and murder on the high seas, within the Jurisdiction of the said United States of America,

on the seventh day of December, inst., are, or some of them are now in the City of Saint John, within this Province, and requesting that the said John C. Braine, H. C. Brooks, David Collins, John Parker Locke, Robert Clifford, Linus Seely, George Robinson, Gilbert Cox, Robert Cox, H. A. Parr, and James McKinney, may be delivered up to Justice according to the Provisions of the said Treaty; such warrant directed to all and every the Justices of the Peace and officers of Justice within the Province of New Brunswick, and is as follows:—Here His. Excellency's Warrant is inserted **Vide Appendix D.**

And whereas on the receipt of the said warrant by me and acting under and by virtue thereof and in pursuance of the said Act of Parliament, I did examine

183

Isaac Willett under oath touching the truth of the said charges set forth in the said warrant and upon the evidence of the said Isaac Willett in pursuance of the said Act of Parliament, I did on the 2oth day of December last, issue my warrant under my band and seal for the apprehension of the said persons upon the charges aforesaid in the words following;—(**Here is inserted warrant of apprehension, vide Appendix F**.)

And David Collins, James McKinney, and Linus Seely, three of the persons in the said warrant, having been found within my jurisdiction and having been arrested and brought before me, under and by virtue of the said warrant, and I having proceeded to the investigation of the charge of piracy charged against the said named persons so brought before me and upon the examination of the witnesses under oath touching the offence of piracy charged against the parties so brought before me, and upon the evidence before me under oath, I do hereby under the Act of the Imperial Parliament command you the said Constable or Peace Officers to convey the said David Collins, James McKinney, and Linus Seely, to the common jail of the City and County of Saint John and deliver each of them to the keeper thereof upon the charge of piracy, for that they having on the seventh day of December in the year of our Lord one thousand eight hundred and sixty-three on the high seas about twenty miles north north east of Cape Cod in the United States of America, with force and arms, maliciously, willfully, feloniously, and piratically made an assault upon the said Isaac Willett and others, the mariners then on board and in charge and command of the steamboat or vessel named the *Chesapeake*, the said vessel being a vessel belonging to the United States of America and registered in the United States, according to the laws of such States and belonging to one Henry B.

184

Cromwell, a citizen of the United States of America, and being of the value of sixty thousand dollars of lawful money of New Brunswick, and having on board a cargo of the value of eighty thousand dollars of like lawful money, and the said vessel being then on a voyage from the port of New York in the United States of America, to the port of Portland in the said United States of America, and having then and there piratically, feloniously, willfully, and maliciously put the said Isaac Willett and others, the crew of the said vessel, in fear and danger of their lives on the high seas aforesaid, and having then and there maliciously, willfully, feloniously, and piratically taken possession of the said vessel and the cargo thereof, and with having then and there feloniously stolen and taken the said vessel and cargo upon the high seas aforesaid, there to remain until delivered pursuant to the requisition as aforesaid. And you the said keeper shall receive and safely keep each of them upon the said charge until delivered pursuant to such requisition as aforesaid.

Given under my hand and seal at the City of Saint John, in the City and County of Saint John, this twenty-fifth day of February, in the year of our Lord one thousand eight hundred and sixty-four.

(Signed) H. T. GILBERT, *a Justice of the Peace for the City and County of St. John and Police Magistrate for said City.*

And this is the cause of the detaining the said David Collins, James McKinney, and Linus Seely, whose bodies I have ready.

26th *February,* 1864.

JAMES A. HARDING, *Sheriff of the City*

and County of Saint John

The summary from records of the U. S. Navy:

Chesapeake was the wooden steamer *Totten,* built in Philadelphia in 1853 and first registered there. She was rebuilt in 1857, being renamed *Chesapeake* 27 August and described at that time as schooner-rigged with single funnel, owned by H. B. Cromwell & Co., New York. She was involved in the *Caleb Cushing* (q.v.) affair in June 1863, being one of the ships that set out from Portland, Me., to recapture the revenue cutter.

She was sailing as a regular New York-Portland liner on 7 December 1863 when she became a cause celebre upon being taken over as a Confederate vessel by a group acting in the name of the Confederacy under alleged authority of a second-hand letter of marque issued 27 October to the former captain of a privateer sold as unseaworthy in Nassau some months earlier—whereas her relief captain, mastermind of this later expedition, was found to be a British subject, having acted under an assumed name and without authorization by the Confederacy. The Halifax, N.S., Court of Vice-Admiralty found, 15 February 1864, that the capture "was undoubtedly a piratical taking. But in its origin, in the mode of the recapture, in short, all the concomitant circumstances, the case is very peculiar."

Chesapeake was restored to her owners and served in commerce until 1881.

The captors were dismissed: "This court has no prize jurisdiction, no authority to adjudicate between the United States and the Confederate States, or the citizens of either of those States. The prisoners were not surrendered to the United States under the Ashburton treaty for trial" on charges of murder and piracy."

"Colonel" John Clibbon Braine, Henry A. Parr and a dozen fellow-conspirators took over Chesapeake 20 miles NNE of Cape Cod, 7 December, having boarded her two nights before in New York as passengers. In the takeover, her second engineer was killed and her chief officer and chief engineer wounded; Captain Isaac Willett, his bona fide passengers and all but five of his crew were landed at St. John, N.B., 8 December; Capt. John Parker (actually Vernon G. Locke) joined in the Bay of Fundy and took command. They coaled at Shelburne, N.S., the 12th, shipped four men and were seeking enough fuel to make Wilmington, N.C., when *USS Ella & Annie* (v. William G. Hewes) captured *Chesapeake*, the morning of the 17th, in Sambro, a small harbor near the entrance to Halifax, N.S., with three crewmen—only one being of the boarding party.

Comdr. A. G. Clary, *USS Dacotah*, prevented Ella & Annie from taking the recaptured prize into Boston and accompanied her that day to Halifax, where she was turned over to local authorities the 19th—conceding that her recovery in neutral waters of Canada had been extra-legal—and the prisoners with her.

Eight Federal ships hastily summoned to search out *Chesapeake* returned home the 19th; the same day Secretary of State J. P. Benjamin appointed James B. Holcombe special commissioner to represent the alleged Confederate raiders in Halifax and try to gain possession of the prize steamer. Holcombe found ultimately, "That the expedition was devised, planned, and organized in a British colony by Vernon G. Locke, a British subject, who, under the feigned name of Parker, had been placed in command of the privateer *Retribution* by the officer who was named as her commander at the time of the issue of the letter of marque.

189

Locke assumed to issue commissions in the Confederate service to British subjects on British soil, without authority for so doing, and without being himself in the public service of this Government.

There is great reason to doubt whether either Braine, who was in command of the expedition, or Parr, his subordinate, is a Confederate citizen.

Braine after getting possession of the vessel and proceeding to the British colonies, instead of confining himself to his professed object of obtaining fuel for navigating her to a Confederate port, sold portions of the cargo at different points on the coast, thus divesting himself of the character of an officer engaged in the legitimate warfare.

The capture of the *Chesapeake*, therefore, is disclaimed.

"Men who, sympathizing with us in a righteous cause, erroneously believed themselves authorized to act as belligerents against the United States by virtue of Parker's possession of the letter of marque issued to the privateer Retribution" could not be accepted after the fact as Confederate volunteers.

Ella and Annie

USS *Malvern*, a 1477-ton (burden) iron side-wheel gunboat, was built in 1860 as the commercial steamship *William G. Hewes*. She later became a Confederate blockade runner, was renamed *Ella and Annie* and on 9 November 1863 was captured by *USS Niphon* while attempting to enter the port of Wilmington, North Carolina.

Soon purchased by the U.S. Navy, she was briefly commissioned under the name *Ella and Annie* in December 1863 to search for the captured steamship *Chesapeake*. After finding and seizing that vessel in Nova Scotia waters, *Ella and Annie* returned to the Boston Navy Yard to complete her conversion to a warship. Commissioned in February 1864 as USS *Malvern*, she was employed for much of the remainder of the Civil War as flagship of the North Atlantic Blockading Squadron. As such, she was present during the capture of Fort Fisher, North Carolina, in January 1865 and received credit for

191

the subsequent capture of the blockade running steamers *Charlotte* and *Stag*. During the next month *Malvern* took part in operations on the Cape Fear River, N.C., and was active in the James River area of Virginia as the Civil War neared its end. Following the fall of Richmond, Va., in early April 1865, she transported President Abraham Lincoln up the James to visit that city, the former capital of the Confederacy.

In October 1865, some six months after the war's conclusion, USS *Malvern* was sold at auction. She soon regained her original name, *William G. Hewes*, and in early 1866 began what was to be nearly three more decades of commercial employment. On 20 February 1895 the old steamship was wrecked during a storm off the Cuban coast.

--- United States Naval Historical Center

Part Three

Mutiny of the HMS Hermione and Bloody Acts of Murder

While Mutiny on the Bounty has become the iconic Hollywood depiction of a mutiny on the High Seas, the mutiny which took place on the HMS Hermione was far bloodier.

The trial records of the bloodiest Mutiny of a Royal Navy vessel are contained among the records of the United States District Court of New Jersey and are provided to the reader as the only contemporaneous record of the murder of much of the crew, at the hands of fellow crew members. Twenty-four of the crew was later hanged by the British. Three of the crew were captured and held by the United States, which returned them to the British under a treaty which returned criminals to each nation from the other.

Another of the mutineers, Jonathan Robbins, who was also known as Thomas Nash, was held in an American jail before being determined by Judge Thomas Bee to not be an American citizen. He was promptly turned over the British under the terms of the Jay Treaty, which took him to Jamaica and hanged him on Aug. 19, 1799. The incident incited a Virginia law which prohibited extraditions and soon Virginia ports were overrun with desertions from British ships. The times were turbulent for the young republic which had just won its independence from Britain. The issue sparked a debate over the executive powers of the president that has continued to modern times. The court records of three of those who were held in New Jersey show clearly the intercession of the President John Adams in the indictments brought against three of the mutineers in what would have been a landmark case had it gone forward.

The controversy spilled over into the elections that year with Congressman John Marshall of Virginia defending President Adams' action: Congressman John Marshall declared that "the President is the sole organ of the nation in its external relations, and its sole representative with foreign nations. Of consequence the demand of a foreign nation can only be made on him."

Adams, in one of his last acts as President, appointed Marshall Chief Justice of the Supreme Court, where he would sit as the longest serving Chief Justice in United States history. Ironically, Marshall also sat on the trial of three Spaniards in 1826 in Federal Court in

Richmond, Virginia, who were captured in Norfolk after participating in a the piracy of a vessel.

The *HMS Hermione* was a 32-gun fifth-rate frigate of the Royal Navy which was launched in 1782 at Bristol, England. The HMS Hermione was the first of six such ships in its class and was captured by mutineers on Sept. 27, 1797, was sold by the crew to the Spanish which renamed it the Santa Cecilia. It was captured by the Royal Navy on Sept. Oct. 25, 1799 and renamed the *HMS Retaliation* and later named the *Retribution* on January 31, 1800. The ship was sold for scrap in 1805.

The *HMS Hermione* had a draft of 9 feet 2 inches, was 129 feet in length and had a beam of 35 feet and 5' ½". With a full crew of 220, the ship was powered by sails.

Capt. Hugh Pigot was especially cruel for a commanding officer of his day, handing out severe punishments for minor infractions, even to his officers. The *HMS Hermione* had been patrolling waters off of Puerto Rico in the Mona Passage in 1797 and had sunk three privateers. With several other British warships, the *HMS Mermaid, HMS Drake, HMS Penelope and HMS Quebec*, the *Hermione* had been victorious at the Battle of Jean-Rabel over nine ships at no loss of any crew. On Sept. 6th, the *HMS Hermione* captured a Spanish ship with troops on board.

When an officer was humiliated in front of the crew by being given 12 lashes over the failure of one his crewmen to properly fasten a sail, the die was cast on what would eventually lead to a bloody battle to take over the ship. More cruelty by Capt. Pigot over harsh punishment led to three sailors rushing down from the masts but falling to their deaths. Their bodies were ordered tossed overboard while the Captain cursed them. When sailors complained over the act, half of them were then flogged.

By the evening of Sept. 21st, 1797, the awful chain of events culminated in an attack on the Captain's cabin with the guard quickly being eliminated. Sabers and long knives were used to carve up the cruel Captain in a process that envisions some of the pain he had administered being slowly and viciously returned. It was said that the mutineers responded to his pleas for mercy by stating that he had shown no mercy to his crew and therefore deserved none.

Pigot's dead body was thrown overboard and the mutineers soon had murdered another eight of the Hermione's officers and all of the dead were thrown overboard.

In heroic action at Puerto Cabello, Venezuela, Capt. Edward Hamilton recaptured the Hermione from the Spanish even though his ship was vastly outgunned. He was knighted for his valor and his ship *'Surprise'* was aptly named.

A Pirate's Ruse

*Circuit Court of the United States, Middle
Circuit of the New-Jersey District*

Indictment for murder

The United States, v. William Brigstock, otherwise,
called John Johnston

A true Bill.

B. SMITH, *Foreman*

The defendant being charged on this indictment,
pleaded not guilty

R. BOGGS, *Clerk*

LUCIUS HORATIO STOCKTON,
Attorney. U. S. N. J. District

*Circuit Court of the United States,
New-Jersey District, to wit,*

THE jurors and affirmants, in behalf of the United
States of America, for the body of New-Jersey district, of
the middle circuit, upon their respective oath and
affirmation, present, That William Brigstock, otherwise
called John Johnston, late of the Kingdom of Great
Britain, mariner, not having the fear of God before his
eyes, but being moved and seduced by the instigation of
the devil, on or about the twentieth day of September, in
the year of our Lord one thousand seven hundred and

ninety-seven, with force and arms upon the high seas, near the coast of the island of Porto Rico, in the West Indies, and out of the jurisdiction of any particular state of the United States, and within the jurisdiction of this court, in and on board a certain armed frigate or vessel, called the *Hermione* (whereof a certain Hugh Pigot was then commander) then and there being, feloniously, willfully, and of his malice aforethought, did make an assault in and upon one Foreshaw, one of the lieutenants then and there being on board of said armed frigate or vessel, in the peace of God and of the United States, then and there being, and to the armed frigate and vessel aforesaid, called the *HMS Hermione*, then and there belonging, and that the aforesaid William Brigstock, otherwise called John Johnston, with a certain **tomahawk** of the value of eight-pence, which he the said William Brigstock,' otherwise called John Johnston, then and there had **and held in his right hand, did violently, feloniously, piratically, willfully, and of his malice aforethought, beat and strike the aforesaid Foreshaw in and upon the right side of the head of the said Foreshaw**, he the said Foreshaw then and there being on the high seas, in the armed frigate or vessel aforesaid, and within the jurisdiction of this court aforesaid, giving the said Foreshaw then and there, **with the tomahawk aforesaid**, in and upon the right part of the head aforesaid, of him the said Foreshaw, one mortal bruise, of which mortal bruise the aforesaid Foreshaw, from the said twentieth day of September, in the year aforesaid, until the twenty-first day of the said month of September, in the year aforesaid, upon the high seas aforesaid, in the armed frigate or vessel aforesaid, and within the jurisdiction aforesaid, did languish, and languishing did live, on which twenty-first day of September, in the year aforesaid, he, the said Foreshaw, on the high seas aforesaid, near the aforesaid coast of Porto Rico, in the West Indies aforesaid, in the armed frigate or vessel aforesaid, called the **HMS Hermione**, without the jurisdiction of any particular state of the United States, and within the jurisdiction of this court aforesaid, *did die;* and so the jurors and affirmants aforesaid, upon their oath and affirmation aforesaid, do say, that the aforesaid William Brigstock, otherwise called John Johnston, him the said Foreshaw, upon the high seas aforesaid, in the armed frigate or vessel aforesaid, and within the jurisdiction of this court aforesaid, in manner and form aforesaid, feloniously, *piratically,* willfully, and of his malice aforethought, did kill and murder, against the peace of the United States, and against the form of the statute in such case made and provided.

LUCIUS HORATIO STOCKTON,
Attorney for the United States for the New-Jersey District

ENDORSED.

Circuit Court of United States, Middle Circuit New-Jersey District
BY the special command of the President of the United States, a *nolle prosequi* is entered on this indictment the twenty-eighth day of June, in the year of our Lord one thousand seven hundred and ninety-eight.

LUCIUS HORATIO STOCKTON,
200

*Attorney of the United States for the
New-Jersey District*

I CERTIFY the foregoing, together with the endorsement, on the back or outside of this paper, to be truly copied from the original indictment remaining on file in my office.

ROBERT BOGGS,
Clerk of the said court.
March 1st, 1800.

Circuit Court of the United States, Middle 7 Circuit of the New-Jersey District
The United States,
(v.)
William Brigstock, otherwise called John Johnston, John Evans, otherwise called Michael Campbell, and Joannes Williams, otherwise called Joannes Williamson

**Indictment
for
Piracy.**

**A true Bill
B. SMITH, Foreman:**
The defendant being charged on this indictment, pleaded not guilty.

R.BOGGS, Clerk

LUCIUS HORATIO STOCKTON,
Attorney U. S. N. J. District

Circuit Court of the United States, 7
New-Jersey District, to wit,

THE jurors and affirmants, in behalf of the United States of America, for the body of New-Jersey District of the Middle Circuit, upon their respective oath and affirmation, present. That **William Brigstock,** otherwise called John Johnston, **John Evans,** otherwise called Michael Campbell, and **Joannes Williams**, otherwise called Joannes Williamson, late of the Kingdom of Great Britain, mariners**, on the twentieth day of September, in the year of our Lord one thousand seven hundred and ninety-seven**, with force and arms, and so forth, upon the high seas, and out of the jurisdiction of any particular state of the United States, and within the jurisdiction of this court, to wit, about ten leagues from Porto Rico in the West Indies, in parts beyond the seas, then being mariners in and on board a certain armed frigate or vessel, called the *Hermione*, **belonging and appertaining to the King of Great Britain,** whereof one **Hugh Pigot**, a subject of the said King of Great Britain, was *then* and there commander, **did betray the trust in them reposed as mariners of the said armed frigate** or vessel, and then and there, out of the jurisdiction of any particular state of the United States as aforesaid, upon the high seas aforesaid, and within the jurisdiction of this court aforesaid, **with force and arms did turn pirates,** and the same armed frigate or vessel, and the apparel and tackle thereof, of the value of fifty thousand dollars lawful money of the United States, and one silver tankard, of the value of fifty dollars like money, and one gold watch of the value of one bunked dollars of the money, and one silver spoon of; the value of two dollars of like money, of

202

the goods and chattels of certain subjects of the said King of Great Britain (to the Jurors and affirmants aforesaid yet unknown) then and there being in the said armed frigate or vessel, called the **HMS *Hermione***, under the care and custody of the said Hugh Pigot, as commander thereof, then and there, upon the high seas we said, without the jurisdiction of any particular state of the United States as aforesaid, and within the jurisdiction of this court as aforesaid, with force and, arms from the care, custody and possession of the said Hugh Pigot, piratically, and feloniously did run away with (they the said William Brigstock, otherwise called John Johnston, John Evans, otherwise called Michael Campbell and Joanne Williams, otherwise called Joannes Williamson, then and there being mariners of the said armed frigate or vessel, and in and on board the same, on the high seas aforesaid against the peace of the United States, and against the form of the statute in such cafe made and provided.

LUCIUS HORATIO STOCKTON,
Attorney of the United States for the
District of New Jersey.

I CERTIFY the foregoing, together with the Endorsement on the back hereof, to be truly copied from the original indictment remaining on file in my office.

ROBERT BOGGS,
Clerk of the said court,

March 1st, 1800.
Circuit Court of the United States, Middle'
Circuit of the New-Jersey District of

The United States,

203

v.

William Brigstock, otherwise called
John Johnston,

Indictment for piracy.
A true Bill.

B. SMITH, *Foreman.*
Circuit-Court of the United States of New-Jersey
District to wit,

THE jurors and affirmants, in behalf of the United States of America, for the body of New-Jersey District of the middle circuit, upon their respective oath and affirmation, present, That William Brigstock, otherwise called John Johnston, being a citizen of the State of New York, one of the United States of America, late of the Kingdom of Great Britain, mariner, on the twentieth day of September, in the year of our Lord one thousand seven hundred and ninety-seven, with force and arms, and so forth, upon the high seas, and out of the jurisdiction of any particular state of the United States, and within the jurisdiction of this court, to wit, about ten leagues from Porto Rico in the West Indies, in parts beyond the seas, then being a mariner, to wit, the boatswain's mate in and on board a certain armed frigate or vessel, called the Hermione, belonging and appertaining to the king of Great Britain, whereof one Hugh Pigot, a subject of the said king of Great Britain, was then and there commander, did betray the trust in him reposed as a mariner, to wit, the boatswain's mate of the said armed frigate or vessel, and then and there out of the jurisdiction of any particular state of the United States, as aforesaid, upon the high seas aforesaid, and within the jurisdiction of this court aforesaid, with force and arms (together with divers other persons

204

whose names are not at present known to the jurors and affirmants aforesaid) did turn a pirate, and the fame armed frigate or vessel, and the apparel and tackle thereof, of the value of fifty thousand dollars, lawful money of the United States, and one silver tankard of the value of fifty dollars like money, and one gold watch of the value of one hundred dollars of like money, and one silver spoon of the value of two dollars of like money, of the goods and chattels of the said Hugh Pigot, and of other subjects of the said King of Great Britain, to the jurors and affirmants aforesaid as yet unknown, then and there being in the said armed frigate or vessel, called the Hermione, under the care and custody of the said Hugh Pigot, as commander thereof, then and there upon the high seas aforesaid, without the jurisdiction of any particular state of the United States, as aforesaid, with force and arms, and so forth, from the care, custody and possession of the said Hugh Pigot, piratically and feloniously did run away with the said William Brigstock, otherwise called John Johnston, a citizen of the state of New-York, one of the United States of America, as aforesaid, then and there being a mariner, to wit, the boatswain's mate of the said armed frigate or- vessel, and in and on board the fame on the high seas aforesaid) against the peace of the United States, and against the form of the statute in such case made and provided.

LUCIUS HORATIO STOCKTON
Attorney of the United States,
For the
New Jersey District Circuit Court of United States,
Middle Circuit, New-Jersey

BY the Special command of the President of the United States, a *nolle prosequi* is entered on this indictment Twenty-eighth of June, A. D. 1798

LUCIUS HORATIO STOCKTON,

Attorney of the United States for the New-Jersey District

I CERTIFY the foregoing, together with the endorsement on the back hereof, to be truly copied from the original indictment remaining on file in my office.

ROBERT BOGGS,

Clerk of the said Court,
March 1st, 1800.

COPIES OF HABEUS CORPUS.

Answer and Commitment.

Middle circuit court of New-Jersey district.

-**The president of the United States of America**, to the keeper of the common goal or prison of the county of Middlesex, in the New-Jersey district, greeting:

You are hereby commanded, that the bodies of William Brigstock, alias John Johnston, Johannes Williamson, alias Johan Jacob Williamson and Michael Campbell alias John Evans, in your prison detained ; as is said, under a safe and secure conduct, together with the day and cause of their caption and detention, by whatsoever names they may be called, in the fame you have before the justices of the circuit court of the United States, at the circuit court now holden before the justices aforesaid at Trenton ; in and for the New-Jersey district on Thursday the fifth day of April instant, to do, receive and submit to, what the said justices shall then and there confider concerning them and each of them in this behalf: and have you then and there this writ. Witness, Oliver Elfworth, Esq. Chief justice at Trenton, the second day of April, in the year of our Lord one thousand seven hundred and ninety eight.

R. BOGGS, Clerk

L. H. Stockton. District Attorney

ANSWER.

The answer of Peter Keenon, the keeper of the common jail or prison of the county of Middlesex in the New Jersey district to the writ hereunto this schedule is annexed.

The bodies of William Brigstock alias John Johnston, Johannes Williamson, alias Johan Jacob Williamson, and Michael Campbell, alias John Evans, the persons in the fame writ named. I have before the court at the time and place within mentioned, for the purposes therein contained, and the day and cause of their caption and detainer, I do hereby certify to be contained in the warrant of commitment hereunto annexed.

Witness my hand this fifth day of April, A.D. 1798.

P. KEENON.

COMMITMENT.

State of New-Jersey city of Perth Amboy

The State of New-Jersey, to the marshal of the said city, and to the keeper of the jail at New Brunswick in the county of Middlesex greeting: Whereas Johannis Williamson, John Johnston and Michael Campbell, mariners on board the brig relief, now lying in the port of Perth Amboy aforesaid, **have been arrested for suspicion of felony by them, as it is said, committed, in feloniously murdering on the high seas, the captain and other officers of his Britannic Majesty's ship the** *Hermione*, **and together with the rest of the crew of the said ship piratically delivering up the said ship** *Hermione* **to the officers of the King of Spain,** now at war with his said Britannic Majesty.

And whereas it is stipulated in the treaty of amity and commerce between the United States and Great Britain, that persons committing murder or piracy in one of the said countries or within its jurisdiction, **shall not receive protection or refuge in the other.**

We therefore command you the said marshal forthwith to convey and deliver into the custody of the said keeper of the jail aforesaid, the bodies of the said Johannis Williamson, John Johnston and Michael Campbell, and you the said keeper are hereby required to receive the said Johannis Williamson, John Johnston and Michael Campbell into your custody in the said jail, and them safely keep until they are delivered by due course of law, or removed by the proper authority. Given under our hands and seals at Perth Amboy in the county of Middlesex, the tenth day of March, A. D. 1798.

ANDREW BELL, Recorder.
JOHN RATTOONE, Alderman

I certify the foregoing to be truly copied from the original habeas corpus answer, and commitment, remaining on file in my office.

March 1, 1800
ROBERT BOGGS, Clerk
of the said court.

Circuit Court of United States New Jersey District.
Copy of Minutes.

I certify the within to be truly copied from the Minutes of the Circuit Court of the United States, in and for New Jersey District.

ROBERT BOGGS,
Clerk of said Court.

209

March 1, 1800. ,

COPY OF MINUTES.

Circuit Court of the United States held at Trenton in and for New-Jersey district on Wednesday the fourth day of April, in the year of our Lord one thousand seven hundred and ninety eight.

Present the Hon. Samuel Chase, esquire,
Justice of the United States Supreme Court,
Robert Morris esquire,
District Judge.

The United States,
vs.
William Brigstock,
alias **John Johnston,**
Johannis Williamson
alias
John Jacob Williamson,
and Michael Campbell,
alias
John Evans. J

The defendants being confined on a charge of piracy, in the common goal of the county

Of Middlesex; on motion of the district attorney, ordered that a Habeas Corpus, do exist, directed to the jailer of the said prison commanding him to bring into this bodies of the said defendants

Thursday 5th April, 1798.

Frances Martin, sworn as a witness to go before the grand jury.

210

Friday, 6th April, 1798

The grand jury came into court and being called over, they all appeared, and being asked if they had anything to offer to the court, they presented the following bills of indictment.

The United States, vs. William Brigstock,
otherwise called John Johnston,
Indictment for murder on the High Seas

The United States vs. The same.
Indictment for piracy.

The United States,
vs.
William Brigstock, j
alias
John Johnston,
John Evans,
Alias
Michael Campbell,
Joannes Williams,
alias I
Joannes Williamson.
Indictment for piracy

The court being informed by the district attorney that a traverse jury will be wanted to try several criminals, on indictments for Capital offences, ordered that one be legally summoned accordingly.

Monday, 9th April, 1798
The United States, ^
vs.
William Brigstock,
alias **John Johnston,**
John Evans,
alias **Michael**
Campbell,
Joannes Williams,
alias
Joannes Williamson.

Indictment for piracy.

On motion of the district attorney, ordered that the prisoner be set to the bar that the marshal return the venire in this cause, and that the trial thereof come on
—Whereupon the following persons, were sworn and affirmed after all challenges on the jury, viz.
1 Ellet Tucker
2 John Morris, Jr.
3 Albemarle Collins,
4 Joshua Newbold,
5 Joseph Brumley,
6 Smith Hill,
7 John Bellerjeau, Jr.
8 Samuel Bellerjeau,
9 William Smith,
10 Joseph McCulley
11 Enoch Cook,
12 Mahlon Reed.

For United States,
Lucius H. STOCKTON,

District Attorney.
William Griffith, counsel.
Witness
Frances Marten, Sworn.

For the Defendants,
Samuel Leatre and Aaron D. Woodruff
Counsel for Defendants
Witness for Defendants
Samuel Lay, Ann Huet
John Bayley, Robert Boggs
Richard Soderstrom,
Thos. Lowrey.

The counsel summed up to the jury, and Judge Chase charged them, when they withdrew to consider of their verdict, with a constable sworn to attend them.

Court adjourned for an hour, and met again pursuant to adjournment.

The jury came into Court, and being called over, they all appeared, and being asked if they had agreed on their verdict, they said they had, and by their Foreman, Ellet Tucker said they found the prisoners at the Bar, William Brigstock alias, John Johnston, John Evans alias, Michael Campbell, and Joannes Williams alias, Joannes Williamson, and each of them, not guilty of the charge whereof they stand indicted respectively, and so they said all.

The Court order, that William Brigstock, alias John Johnston, be committed to the safe and close custody of the Marshal of the District, there to remain, until thence delivered by due course of Law.

In October Sessions 1798,

Present the Honorable William Cushing Esq. one of the Justices of the Supreme Court;

Robert Morris Esq.

District Judge.

The United States of America

Vs. William Brigstock

On indictment for murder, I will no further prosecute the above indictment.

Lucius HORATIO STOCKTON,
Attorney of the United States for
the New-Jersey District.

Take notice that in obedience to the special command of the President of the United States, I have this day entered a nolle prosequi, on each of the above Indictments, and that it is the pleasure of the President of the United States, that the prisoner be discharged from your custody; and from answering further, or from being further held on the above indictments, or either of them. Dated at Trenton this 28th. of June A. D. 1798.

I am Sir, Your Obedient Servant.

To Thomas Lowry Efqr.

Marshal of the district of N. J. or Thomson Stelle, Esq. one of his deputies, or to the keeper of the common prison in the city of New Brunswick in the district of New Jersey, or to any or either of them.

LUCIUS HORATIO STOCKTON,
Attorney of the United States for the
New Jersey district.

I certify the above to be a true copy of a notice remaining, on file ,in my office.

ROBERT BOGGS, Clerk
of the said Court.
March 1st. 1800.

Post Script: The outcome of this action is that the three prisoners were released to the Royal Navy and a total of 24 of the mutineers were hanged.

The End

Ken Rossignol at the Titanic Museum Attraction in Branson, Missouri during a book signing.

About the Author:

After covering hard news for 22 years while publishing a weekly newspaper, Rossignol sold the newspaper in 2010 and has begun devoting full time to writing and is now the author of fourteen books.

As a maritime history speaker, Rossignol enjoys meeting audiences around the world and discussing the original news stories of the sinking of the RMS Titanic and other maritime history topics.

In 2012 Rossignol has appeared on nine ships in the Pacific, Atlantic and Caribbean discussing the stories of the heroes of the Titanic, the explorations of the new world voyagers, the Bermuda Triangle and the history of piracy.

Rossignol appears at the Titanic Museum Attractions in Pigeon Forge, Tennessee and Branson, Missouri for book signings and to talk with visitors about the RMS Titanic.

He has appeared on Good Morning America, ABC 20/20; ABC World News Tonight and in a 2012 production of Discovery Channel Investigation Motives & Murders Series, A Body in the Bay.

News coverage of Rossignol's landmark civil rights case, represented by Levine Sullivan Koch & Schulz re: United States Fourth Circuit Court of Appeals *Rossignol v Voorhaar*, 2003, included articles in most major news outlets, as well as a column by syndicated columnists James J. Kilpatrick.

The story of the *St. Mary's Today* newspaper is now available in ebook and paperback: *The Story of THE RAG!* The book includes nearly 200 editorial cartoons that appeared over the years.

A strong highway safety advocate, Rossignol also publishes the DWIHitParade.com which focuses on impaired driving and the monthly publication, *The Chesapeake.*

News coverage of Rossignol's DWIHitParade won an Emmy in 2012 for WJLA reporter Jay Korff and coverage of the St. Mary's Today newspaper by WUSA reporter Bruce Leshan was awarded an Emmy in 2000.

Available in paperback and ebooks

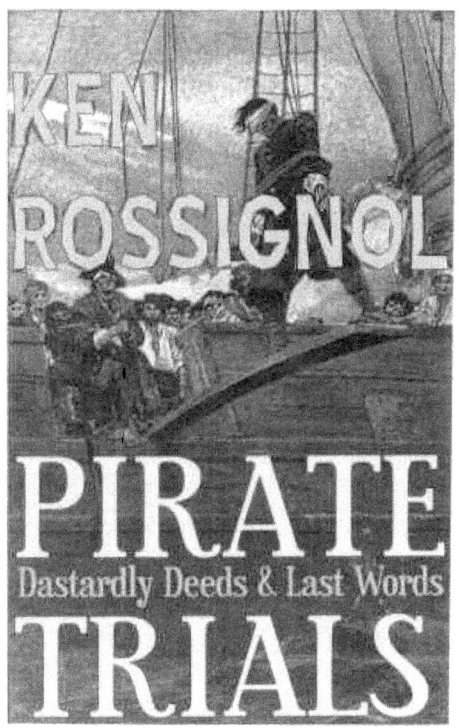